The Contrast

The Contrast

Manners, Morals, and Authority in the
Early American Republic

Cynthia A. Kierner

NEW YORK UNIVERSITY PRESS
New York and London

NEW YORK UNIVERSITY PRESS
New York and London
www.nyupress.org

Tyler, Royall, 1757–1826
The contrast : manners, morals, and authority in the early
American republic / [edited by] Cynthia A. Kierner.
p. cm.
A reprint of The contrast by Royall Tyler, with annotated
footnotes and an extensive introduction; also features selections
from contemporary letters, essays, novels, conduct books, and
public documents, which debate issues of the era.
Includes bibliographical references and index.
ISBN-13: 978-0-8147-4792-6 (cloth : acid-free paper)
ISBN-10: 0-8147-4792-2 (cloth : acid-free paper)
ISBN-13: 978-0-8147-4793-3 (pbk. : acid-free paper)
ISBN-10: 0-8147-4793-0 (pbk. : acid-free paper)
1. New York (N.Y.)—Social life and customs—18th century—
Drama. 2. Manners and customs—Drama. 3. Conduct of life—
Drama. 4. Betrothal—Drama. 5. Arranged marriage—Drama.
6. Mate selection—Drama. 7. Politics and literature—United
States—History—18th century—Sources. 8. United States—
Intellectual life—1783–1865—Sources. I. Kierner, Cynthia A.,
1958–ￜ II. Title.
PS855.T7C6 2007
812'.1—dc22   2006035521

New York University Press books are printed on acid-free paper,
and their binding materials are chosen for strength and durability.

Manufactured in the United States of America
c 10 9 8 7 6 5 4 3 2 1
p 10 9 8 7 6 5 4 3 2 1

Contents

Illustrations

Preface

On 14 April 1787, a small notice—thirty-eight words, no pictures—appeared on one of the inside pages of New York's *Daily Advertiser*. This brief newspaper notice advertised the imminent performance of a new five-act comedy called *The Contrast*. It also informed readers that the play had been "written by a Citizen of the United States." The playwright's country of origin was clearly more significant than his specific identity, which the notice did not disclose. Some readers, however, already knew that the author was Royall Tyler, a visitor from Massachusetts. The premier of Tyler's comedy, *The Contrast,* at New York's only theater on 16 April, would be a notable occasion, the first professional production of a play written by an American.

The Contrast appealed to patriots and nationalists who championed the creation of a distinctive American culture, while addressing timely issues of critical importance to post-revolutionary Americans. As they fought for and won their independence from Great Britain, Americans embarked on a republican experiment that they believed would turn out fundamentally different from—and, in their view, superior to—European monarchies. As they did so, they pondered the sorts of manners, morals, education, and leadership that would be most compatible with their often conflicting interpretations of republican political values. A New England patriot, Royall Tyler wrote *The Contrast* in part to explore the much vaunted differences between republican simplicity and transparency, on the one hand, and European-style ostentation and duplicity, on the other, and to ask whether Americans' rejection of monarchy in 1776 in truth necessitated the eradication of all European social forms. *The Contrast* is important not only as a "first" in United States literary history, but also as a barometer of this lively contemporary cultural dialog.

But today's readers also will find timeless themes and issues in *The Contrast,* a comedy of manners in which the main characters are young people. Sex, seduction, fashion, and amusement are at the center of the lives of these characters, whose stories Tyler dramatizes in order to prod his audience into thinking about the sorts of ideals and conduct Americans should value. So, too, is education a key theme in Tyler's play as parents, books, and role models (both positive and negative) influence the conduct and demeanor of his characters. *The Contrast* also explores gender ideals, family relationships, courtship, and marriage, all of which are topics that are as relevant to modern readers as they were to post-revolutionary Americans.

This edition of *The Contrast* is based on that published in New York by the Dunlap Society in 1887, which, in turn, replicated the original Philadelphia edition of 1790. (Although Tyler wrote *The Contrast* in 1787, three years passed before the play appeared in print.) This present edition of Tyler's text includes new annotation to enhance modern readers' understanding of the play, as well as an introductory essay that situates the play in its proper historical context.

The book's concluding section features pairs of contemporary documents that express divergent or opposing views on issues Tyler's plays addresses: the appropriate uses of the arts, literature, and fashion in a republic; the respective attributes of ideal wives and husbands; the purpose of manners and education among a republican people; and the meaning of equality for post-revolutionary Americans. Finally, a brief bibliography offers readers suggestions for further reading on these and other related topics.

The Contrast is a lively introduction to New York's social life in 1787 and, more generally, to a significant subset of the world the revolutionaries made. Happily, Deborah Gershenowitz, my superb editor at New York University Press, shares my sense of history and my sense of humor (this play is funny, too!); I am grateful for her wholehearted support for this project from the start. It was a pleasure working with Debbie and her colleagues at NYU, especially Salwa Jabado and Despina Gimbel. Norma Basch, Charlene Boyer Lewis, and Rosemarie Zagarri, the readers for NYU Press, also were enthusiastically supportive, and their suggestions for improving my proposal influenced (in good ways) the finished product. A book about fashion and manners must have pictures, and I thank the Graduate School at the University of North Carolina at Charlotte for the subvention that paid for mine. Finally, and as always, I thank the guys—Tom, Zachary, and Anders—for letting me work, and also for all our great and small adventures.

I

Introduction

In 1786, five years after his stunning victory at Yorktown, George Washington feared for the survival of the American republic. He worried that its people behaved badly, that selfishness jeopardized the achievements of the Revolution, and that the government established under the Articles of Confederation lacked the power to maintain order. For Washington, Shays's Rebellion in western Massachusetts was the most compelling evidence of the "anarchy and confusion" of the postwar years. The hero of the Revolution warned that lawlessness could lead to the reinstatement of monarchy or perhaps even to the loss of independence. "Without some alteration in our political creed," he predicted, "the superstructure we have been seven years raising at the expence of so much blood and treasure, must fall."[1]

Farmers in western Massachusetts who rebelled against their state government that August saw things differently. Captain Daniel Shays and many of his fellow insurgents had fought the British to secure their rights and liberties during the Revolution. Shays himself was a distinguished war veteran. In 1780, however, a new state constitution consolidated political power in the hands of the eastern mercantile elite, whose interests dictated economic policy in Massachusetts during the postwar era. Western farmers revolted because, from their perspective, the state's enforcement of speedy payment of taxes and debts in hard money unfairly benefited selfish speculators and creditors, who profited at the expense of patriotic citizens. Government efforts to enrich the few at the expense of the many, they maintained, unjustly penalized western farmers, some of whom languished in debtors' prison, where, according to one Shaysite declaration, they were "rendered incapable of being serviceable either to themselves or the community."[2]

The profound disagreement between Washington and Shays, both staunch patriots and avowed republicans, was emblematic of a more general debate on the nature of American politics and society in the

1780s. One aspect of that debate, which focused on the powers of government and its authority in relation to citizens, culminated in the writing and ratification of the U.S. Constitution. Another contemporary debate, however, considered more generally the transformative effects of revolutionary republicanism.

If, as most believed, the survival of republics depended on the virtue and public spirit of their citizens, how should Americans manifest and promote virtue in their families and in society? What was the basis of political and cultural authority in a republican polity? Did the American colonists' ultimate rejection of monarchy in 1776 necessitate the subsequent eradication of all European social forms and customs? Should republican families be more egalitarian than their counterparts under monarchical regimes? Should social distinctions be muted? What sorts of manners, amusements, and education were appropriate and beneficial in this post-revolutionary world? In sum, to be a nation, must Americans have a unique identity and culture? Specifically, must they distinguish themselves from Europeans—and, if so, how? These timely questions were at the heart of Royall Tyler's play, *The Contrast,* which opened at the John Street Theatre in New York in April 1787.

In 1787, the United States was at a crossroads, both culturally and politically. On the one hand, 1787 was a banner year for America's cultural nationalists. Poet Joel Barlow published his epic poem, *The Vision of Columbus,* which celebrated George Washington as an American hero and praised the promise and achievements of American writers and artists. Two new magazines, the *American Museum* and the *American Magazine,* commenced publication, and *The Contrast,* by Royall Tyler, became the first American play performed in public by a professional theater company. On the other hand, by 1787, many Americans worried that their existing political institutions were incapable of resolving the problems of the postwar era, though they disagreed about how serious those problems were and how much change they warranted. In May 1787, advocates for sweeping change scored a signal victory when delegates from every state convened in Philadelphia and drafted a controversial constitution to supplant the Articles of Confederation with a much stronger national government.

From their great triumph at Yorktown in 1781 through the ratification of the U.S. Constitution in 1788, Americans experienced political uncertainty, economic dislocation, and social conflict. At the national level, the

```
THEATRE.

On Monday Evening,
        (Never Performed)
      (Being the 16th of April)
WILL  BE  PERFORMED,
A COMEDY of 5 Acts, written by a
CITIZEN of the United States, Called
     The  Contrast,
To which will be added the English BUR-
        LETTA, Called
    M I D A S.
```

Advertisement for *The Contrast*, 1787. This brief notice first appeared in New York's *Daily Advertiser* on 14 April 1787. Identify-
ing the author simply as "a CITIZEN of the United States" signaled
the play's potential appeal to nationalists who championed American arts and literature in the post-revolutionary era.

Confederation government lacked the power both to tax and to enforce
laws—both of which remained the exclusive domains of the sovereign
states—and consequently was unable to repay debts, negotiate credibly
with foreign nations, or protect and promote American trade and commerce. By 1787, some Americans supported the creation of a more pow-
erful central government as the best means of addressing these problems.
Meanwhile, at the state level, politics grew increasingly contentious, as
members of a once dominant gentry elite now shared power with political newcomers of middling social origins. While many Americans applauded the revolutionary achievement of popular government, gentlemen like George Washington resented what they deemed an excess of democracy and disorder in the states. By 1787, such men wanted a stronger
national government insulated from direct popular influence to impose
order, which they believed essential to the preservation of the republic.

Americans united in their commitment to a republic governed by the people's representatives, but they disagreed profoundly on the issue of how democratic (and how egalitarian) their republic ought to be. Two key issues were at the heart of this debate. First, who were "the people" and how much power should they wield? Second, what sorts of political institutions and cultural forms were best suited to the preservation of a republican political order? In the process of addressing these issues, Americans considered the utility of education, literature, and manners in their society. They also reassessed the meaning of gender, race, and social rank, debating the proper roles of women, African Americans, and non-elite white men in their post-revolutionary world.

Before the Revolution, American society was rigidly and unapologetically hierarchical. Property qualifications kept many men from voting and in many colonies representatives from a few leading families held most political offices. Social mobility, though more common than in Europe, was not typical. Generally, sons of laborers expected to become laboring men themselves; sons of gentlemen expected to inherit their fathers' wealth, connections, and political power, and they usually did.

The rhetoric and reality of the Revolution was deeply unsettling to this hierarchical social order. Involvement in pre-revolutionary protests and committees and in the war itself politicized many non-elite men who sought, and received, a share of political power. During the Revolution, most states decreased property qualifications for both voting and office-holding. In addition, voters increasingly held elected officials accountable for their actions, refusing to re-elect those who ignored their concerns and interests and often choosing middling men who shared their interests to represent them politically. While most Americans agreed that a European-style hereditary aristocracy had no place in the United States, some feared the consequences of popular rule, contending that a "natural aristocracy" of educated, experienced, and enlightened men would be the republic's ideal governors.

But social identities were unusually fluid in revolutionary America. People of all social ranks aspired to upward mobility, and the libertarian ideals of the Revolution led many to believe that such mobility was possible. After the war, many Americans moved to the cities or to the northern, western, or southern frontiers to start new lives. Others looked to education as a means to get ahead. In this unstable social environment, even servants saw themselves less as a permanent laboring class than as temporary hired "help."

The revolutionaries' declaration that "all men are created equal" also led African Americans, supported by some sympathetic whites, to press revolutionary leaders to extend the "inalienable" rights of liberty and equality to slaves and free blacks. They made significant, if limited, gains in several states. In 1777, Vermont claimed independence from New York and adopted a constitution that explicitly banned slavery. In 1783, Massachusetts courts declared slavery unconstitutional, effectively abolishing it in that state. Three years earlier, Pennsylvania had passed a law that provided for the gradual emancipation of slaves, and this statute became a model for the other states. New Yorkers nearly enacted a similar law in the 1785–86 legislative session; they eventually did so in 1799. Further south, the challenge to slavery was less successful, though in 1782 a Virginia law empowered individual slaveowners to manumit their bondpeople. Meanwhile, African Americans attempted to forge new identities as free people, though most whites assumed that even free blacks would be relegated to menial occupations and remain their social inferiors.

The revolutionary era also witnessed unprecedented debate on gender issues, though that conversation focused primarily on the roles and status of elite and middling women. For instance, some educated and articulate women, many of whom had participated in the revolutionary movement, expressed their desire for a degree of political inclusion or empowerment after the war was over. Others unsuccessfully challenged the common law doctrine of coverture, under which a wife's rights to own and control property were vested completely in her husband. Efforts to promote improvements in women's education were more productive in part because many Americans increasingly believed that, as one contemporary essayist put it, "Cultivation of the female mind is of great importance, not with respect to private happiness only, but with respect to society at large."[3]

Reassessing the status of American women was part of a larger transatlantic discourse that unfolded over the course of the eighteenth century as enlightened people embraced a culture of feeling or "sensibility." Stimulating the sentiments or emotions of individuals, many increasingly held, inspired them to act in ways that promoted the virtue and happiness of others. Moralists and social critics, who lauded sensibility in men, nonetheless characterized it as a particularly feminine attribute. The notion of women's special propensity for sensibility, in turn, led many to accept and even to champion feminine influence, both at home and in society.

These new sentimental feminine ideals, which had some influence among the colonists, became more salient after the Revolution, as Americans wrestled with the problem of how best to promote virtue among the citizens of their fledgling republic. Convinced that the survival of the republic depended on the virtue of its citizens, some Americans came to appreciate the potential utility of women's education. Educated women, they suggested, could wield gentle, but beneficial, influence over the values, manners, and morals of their husbands and children. This new idealized republican woman was an American variation on the more general contemporary theme of sentimentalized womanhood. Its proponents infused women's customary roles as wives and mothers with new political or public significance, even as they sought to circumscribe women's influence and activities within their households.

Reappraisals of women's abilities and status were part of a more general rethinking of marriage ideals that had begun earlier in the century as part of the emergence of the culture of sensibility. In Europe and in Europe's American colonies, marriages and families were traditionally patriarchal. Authority, not affection, was the customary basis of family relationships, and both law and custom sanctioned the near-absolute authority of men in their households. Presupposing that women were weak, frivolous, and irrational, this patriarchal ideal accordingly mandated that wives be subservient to their husbands. By the eighteenth century, however, many commentators, who now valued women for their supposedly superior sensibility and virtue, rejected this view in favor of one that emphasized a more affectionate and companionate relationship between spouses. One consequence of this change was a decline in parental control over children's marriage choices, as young people sought matches based on affection which would bring them lasting happiness. Though financial considerations remained important, especially for propertied families, purely mercenary matches became increasingly disreputable.

The rise of companionate marriage, in turn, resulted in the emergence and gradual popularization of new gender ideals for both women and men. In a companionate marriage, the ideal wife would be virtuous, modest, affectionate, and loyal. Her main role was to provide wholesome companionship and support for her husband. The ideal husband would be industrious and independent, able to fulfill his responsibilities both to his family and to the wider community. Strong but not tyrannical, this new companionate husband respected his wife and was unashamedly susceptible to the influence of virtuous women.

Post-revolutionary Americans engaged in a lively debate over the reciprocal duties of spouses. Although some continued to defend the traditional patriarchal marriage ideal, the revolutionary experience seems to have accelerated public acceptance of the newer, more affectionate, and more egalitarian husband-wife relationship. American women, many of whom participated in the Revolution and persevered during the long years of war, demonstrated that they were neither weak nor irrational, thereby proving their suitability as companions and partners. Companionate marriage did not eradicate patriarchy, but it nonetheless elevated the status of women. Proponents of companionate marriage saw husbands and wives as partners in the marital enterprise, though in America, as in Europe, few explicitly endorsed the notion that marriage should be a partnership of equals.

Marriage and family life, in general, were compelling topics for Americans, who looked to the domestic sphere to foster virtue and order in their post-revolutionary world. American revolutionaries had challenged traditional authorities that constituted the underpinnings of the colonial social order. They toppled the monarchy and dismantled religious establishments. The departure of the Tories or loyalists—those Americans who remained loyal to King George III after 1776—and widespread migration within the United States during and after the war led to the break-up of many families and communities. Family, community, and church authorities traditionally had monitored the behavior of individuals, imposing significant penalties on those who violated social norms. With the weakening or dissolution of these customary constraints, many Americans looked to affective family bonds to constrain vice and instill virtue in the younger generation.

In the decades before 1776, a combination of cultural and economic factors contributed to a decline in parental authority in colonial America. On the one hand, the same cultural currents that eroded the traditional patriarch's authority over his wife and sentimentalized relations between spouses had a similar effect on relations between parents and children. On the other hand, population growth resulted in land scarcities in some areas, leaving fathers less financially able to provide for their adult children, especially their sons. Young men who found their fathers unable to supply them with the property they needed to get started in life left home, seeking opportunity elsewhere. The decline of fathers' economic power, in turn, diminished their ability to control their children's behavior and lessened parental influence over the marriage choices of both daughters and sons.

The Revolution compounded these economic and cultural trends. Given the contemporary imagery of kings as father figures, the colonists' overthrow of George III represented a dramatic assertion of anti-patriarchal rights. Indeed, some historians see the colonists' war for independence as the culmination of a larger "American revolution against patriarchal authority" in both politics and family life.[4] At the same time, the war and its aftermath presented youngsters with economic challenges and opportunities that often put them beyond the reach of parental control, both physically and psychologically. Young men, many of whom left home for the first time as revolutionary soldiers, settled elsewhere after the war was over.

Americans reassessed relationships between parents and children, as they did those between spouses, in the post-revolutionary era. What were the obligations, they asked, of children toward their parents? Did the duties of sons differ from those of daughters? Although Americans agreed that children should respect and obey their parents, they debated the limits of parental authority and overwhelmingly gave less freedom to daughters than to sons. Most parents hoped that all of their offspring would marry; chastity before marriage was obligatory for women, though not for men. This sexual double standard, which few questioned, led parents to curtail their daughters' freedom and independence to ensure their sexual purity and thereby advance their marital prospects.

While many Americans considered family life essential to the promotion of popular virtue, others looked beyond the family and championed education, in part as an antidote to declining parental authority. Educational reformers, who assumed that a republican polity required an informed citizenry, agreed that basic literacy skills were essential for post-revolutionary Americans. Many also argued that American citizens, who must be hard-working and self-sufficient, needed instruction in arithmetic, bookkeeping, and other practical matters. The most ambitious champions of education during this period, however, also saw schools as social laboratories. Public-spirited leaders, they maintained, should apply curricular formulae in the classroom to produce virtuous citizens.

From Thomas Jefferson, a Virginia deist, to Noah Webster, an orthodox Christian from New England, leading advocates for improved education argued that schooling in the United States should differ from the European model in two important respects. First, it should be practical, rather than ornamental. Second, it should be broadly accessible. In a republic, they maintained, citizens needed skills to be economically self-supporting and sufficiently knowledgeable and civic-minded to participate in political life.

Although efforts to establish public schools were largely unsuccessful in the post-revolutionary era, private schools and academies proliferated, and Americans also showed widespread interest in self-improvement via less formal types of education. As literacy rates rose in the United States after the Revolution, most Americans chose to educate themselves to rise in the world, socially and economically. Although elite and middling youngsters increasingly attended school, other Americans pursued self-education by reading. Meanwhile, even as America's literary nationalists published an array of essays, poems, and plays that aimed to instill virtue and national feeling in their readers, most of their compatriots revealed a strong preference for other less public-minded genres. As the reading habits of Royall Tyler's characters in *The Contrast* suggest, sentimental novels and conduct books were the most popular genres among post-revolutionary Americans.

Eighteenth-century producers of art and literature assumed that their work would have didactic uses, but their specific objectives varied widely. Post-revolutionary intellectuals labored to build a didactic culture that would advance the goals of nation-building within a republican political order. Assuming a reciprocal relationship between politics and the wider culture, they sought to use literature and the arts to construct and promote a collective American national identity. Other cultural producers, by contrast, aimed to show individuals how to survive and thrive in an increasingly fluid social world. Conduct literature taught men (and, to a lesser extent, women) manners that could help them to rise above their social station. Female readers learned to differentiate gentlemen from rakes—and thus how to safeguard their virtue—by immersing themselves in the cautionary tales of sentimental novels.

Although conduct books existed in Western culture since the Renaissance, their readership increased significantly in post-revolutionary America. By disrupting the existing social order and legitimating the idea of upward mobility through personal effort and merit, the Revolution generated an unprecedented demand for self-improvement manuals among literate non-elites. In the colonial period, gentlemen had been the main audience for conduct literature. After the Revolution, the overwhelming majority of conduct books addressed middling readers who sought to acquire the accoutrements of gentility. Refined manners could help a wealthy but otherwise undistinguished man become a self-made gentleman. Mastering the rules of etiquette also could help a striving youth to get ahead, enabling him to win the friendship and respect of those who might advance his prospects.

By the 1780s, conduct books were readily accessible sources of practical education for many ambitious Americans. Most conduct literature that Americans read was the work of British authors, in part because it was cheaper to import or republish works from Britain than to produce American originals. The most popular conduct manuals were secular, not religious, and offered readers specific rules that they could follow to impress others with their urbane worldliness and polite sensibility. Most were penned by authors of middling social origins.

By far the most influential, however, were the published letters of an English aristocrat, Philip Dormer Stanhope, the fourth Earl of Chesterfield. In the 1740s and 1750s, Chesterfield had written a series of letters to his illegitimate son, Philip Stanhope, in which he described what he believed to be the keys to worldly success. Drawing on his own years of experience in English and Continental high society, Chesterfield instructed his son to cultivate refined manners and polite conversation; the best way to get ahead, he intimated, was to ingratiate oneself with prospective patrons. Chesterfield offered young Philip detailed instructions about how to act with various sorts of people in different social situations. In his letters, he consistently emphasized external appearances over internal morality or character, maintaining that, for those who sought prosperity and preferment, the art of pleasing was paramount.

The first American edition of Chesterfield's *Letters to his Son* appeared in 1775. The book, which became an instant bestseller, was reprinted, all or in part, in many editions through the mid-nineteenth century. Although the popularity of the advice of an English aristocrat in the recently independent American republic might seem anomalous, Chesterfield's emphasis on self-improvement through individual effort and self-fashioning appealed to many middling men, who looked to manners—instead of a genteel pedigree or formal education—as an avenue to respectability. At the same time, Chesterfield's amoral approach to behavior was unpalatable to many post-revolutionary Americans, as it was to some contemporary Britons. Particularly objectionable was the earl's utilitarian attitude toward women, who, he advised, were universally vain and thus readily manipulated by charming and ambitious young men.

Although women, too, read conduct literature during this period, more female readers drew their most compelling life lessons from the pages of sentimental novels. These books, which became popular among readers of both sexes in Britain and British America around mid-century, typically recounted stories of innocent young women who were infatuated with, and eventually seduced by, handsome and well-mannered men who appeared to be honorable. Such stories taught their readers that appearances often were deceiving: the novel's heroine invariably became pregnant and, abandoned by her lover, died alone and in disgrace.

Sentimental novels enjoyed transatlantic readership, but their message perhaps was especially salient to female readers in the United States after the Revolution, when traditional social distinctions based on rank, family pedigree, and local ties were less tenable than they had been during the colonial era. Wartime disruptions, coupled with the geographic and social mobility of the postwar era, made individual identities more malleable. In such an environment, impostors and confidence men flourished, and sexual predators posed special dangers for sheltered and unsuspecting young women.

The predominantly female authors of sentimental fiction sought to teach their readers urgent lessons about preserving feminine chastity and virtue. In so doing, they sought both to constrain sexual license and to promote the safety and happiness of their young female readers. Like authors of conduct manuals, contemporary novelists saw themselves as providing education in the ways of the world. Authors of sentimental novels, however, used their stories to enjoin female readers to be vigilant in these perilous times when a rootless and unprincipled man could assume the guise of genteel sensibility, with tragic results. For example, Susanna Haswell Rowson, author of the enormously popular *Charlotte Temple* (1791), saw her protagonist—seduced, impregnated, and abandoned by a British soldier—as a negative role model for her readers, whom she identified as "the many daughters of Misfortune who, deprived of natural friends, or spoilt by a mistaken education, are thrown on an unfeeling world without the least power to defend themselves from the snares not only of the other sex, but from the more dangerous arts of the profligate of their own."[5]

Sentimental novels, unlike the most popular advice books of the era, were overtly moralistic and emotional, as authors sought to arouse the feelings of sensitive readers to feel the pain of the tragic heroine and thereby avoid sharing her fate. Yet these stories, which conservatively upheld the sexual double standard that punished women, but not men, for sexual transgressions and seem extravagantly moralistic to modern readers, were nonetheless regarded as potentially dangerous by many contemporaries. Some critics complained that because it typically involved seduction and romance, sentimental fiction actually corrupted the morals of readers. Others believed that the time women spent reading novels could be used more productively. Some also worried that the popularity of novels written largely by, for, and about women afforded females too much cultural authority.

At a time when gender stereotypes associated men with reason and women with passion, critics warned that women's cultural influence would have dire political consequences. By undermining rationality and virtue, they argued, novels promoted values that were antithetic to reason and also to republicanism. Sentimental novels, after all, focused their readers' attention on individual passions and interests. By doing so, the novelists' stories titillated readers, distracting them from the more public-minded concerns of republican citizenship.

Although sentimental novels and conduct manuals received the lion's share of American readership after the Revolution, public-minded intellectuals nonetheless strove to create art and literature that could stimulate patriotism and national consciousness. Post-revolutionary cultural nationalists responded to two imperatives. First, they sought to educate and improve their fellow citizens and thereby promote what they saw as distinctively American political and cultural values. Second, they hoped to show the world—or, more specifically, skeptical and disparaging Europeans—that American artists could use themes and images from their own history and environment to create great literature and art.

The establishment of magazines that aimed to attract national audiences was one of the most notable cultural phenomena of the 1780s. In September 1786, the *Columbian Magazine, or Monthly Miscellany,* commenced publication in Philadelphia, boasting subscribers in every state. The magazine's editor sought to "furnish novelty, entertainment,

Frontispiece from the *Columbian Magazine, 1789*. Editors of post-revolutionary magazines envisioned a rosy future for the arts and sciences in the United States, as this illustration suggests. A young woman, representing America, enjoys peace, prosperity, and education, while Apollo points to the Temple of Fame, enjoining her to excel: "Science invites; urg'd by the Voice divine, / Exert thy self, 'till every Art be thine." Library of Congress.

and instruction to his readers" and hoped his publication would "be regarded as a contemporary evidence of the progress of literature and the arts among [America's] citizens . . . to shew, that, the source of all improvement and science, a liberal encouragement, was offered, at this early period of her independency, to every attempt for the advancement of knowledge and virtue." Two other Philadelphia-based magazines, the *American Museum* and the *American Magazine,* appeared the following year. Like the magazines' other gentry patrons, George Washington supported such efforts, which he deemed "easy vehicles of knowledge" that could help "preserve the liberty, stimulate the industry and meliorate the morals of an enlightened and free People."[6]

Post-revolutionary periodicals adapted the model of the English genteel literary magazine to new American circumstances. While they may have aimed for a wider readership, the magazines' relatively high prices meant that their editors would present their combination of reprinted English pieces and new American work to a largely elite audience. The magazines typically included pieces on history, science, manners, and marriage, along with American poetry and other original writing. The first issue of the *Columbian Magazine,* for instance, included an excerpt from David Ramsay's *History of the Revolution in South Carolina,* a brief biography of the revolutionary general Nathanael Greene, an address from a leading American agricultural society, and a section devoted to poetry. In sum, these early magazines sought a national audience to advance patriotism, knowledge, and sensibility among men and women and thereby promote a distinctly genteel and literate form of American national identity.

At the same time, American authors undertook larger projects that pondered the significance of the new republic and the best means to preserve it. In the 1770s, Philip Freneau and some others had begun writing epic poems on American themes. "A Poem, on the Rising Glory of America," which Freneau coauthored with future novelist Hugh Henry Brackenridge in 1772, popularized the notion of American exceptionalism. Freneau and Brackenridge saw America as a new and uniquely virtuous world that would produce "Renown characters, and glorious works / Of high invention and of wond'rous art."[7] Such themes would resonate in the work of writers through the post-revolutionary era.

After the Revolution, however, anxiety tempered earlier optimism about the rising glory of America, as writers focused increasingly on the problems of the postwar years. In 1786–87, conservative poets, known collectively as the Connecticut Wits, published *The Anarchiad,* a series of poems that savagely criticized Shays's Rebellion, condemning the insurgent farmers as hypocrites whose lawless pursuit of self-interest endangered the future of the republic and its more patriotic citizens. Other postwar poets and essayists decried the consumption of foreign luxuries and the adoption of European manners and fashions, which they interpreted as evidence of moral and political corruption. Luxury and extravagance angered both those Americans who disliked social inequality and those who resented the genteel aspirations of the upwardly mobile. Despite their profound disagreement on basic issues like democracy and equality, both camps identified luxury with the gratification of private interests and the resulting neglect of citizens' public responsibilities.

Like nationally-minded writers, leading American artists pursued a consciously didactic course in the post-revolutionary years. While portraits painted for private clients remained the primary source of income for American artists, leading painters also undertook projects to inspire national feeling and public spirit in those who viewed them. In doing so, they drew heavily on themes and incidents from American history. Because the Revolution was the defining moment in the story of American republicanism and nationhood, its events and heroes were especially appealing subjects for a rising generation of American painters that included Charles Willson Peale, Gilbert Stuart, and John Trumbull.

The best-known works of these artists glorified the emerging American nation and its leaders. In 1779, Peale portrayed General George Washington as the confident and victorious commander at the Battle of Trenton; in 1797, Stuart created a more somber, but no less commanding, image of President Washington in civilian dress. John Trumbull's *Declaration of Independence* (1787) shows a gathering of well-dressed, orderly, and like-minded gentlemen purposefully deliberating over Jefferson's declaration. Trumbull's painting imagined American nationhood as the product of the consensual actions of great men. This interpretation, which downplayed both divisions among colonial leaders and the important revolutionary contributions of non-elites, reflected the artist's own conservative political views. Years later, amidst the burgeoning nationalism that followed the War of 1812, Congress commissioned Trumbull to create a much larger version of this painting (and three others) to adorn the rotunda of the nation's Capitol.

While cultural nationalists hailed the production of American visual art and literature in the postwar era, the status of the theater was more

The Declaration of Independence, by John Trumbull, 1787. This often reproduced painting shows Congress receiving the Declaration from the committee that drafted it. By depicting distinctly American scenes, Trumbull's history paintings promoted national consciousness. By attributing the birth of the nation to the decorous actions of a few gentlemen, however, he fostered a conservative and elitist understanding of the Revolution. Yale University Art Gallery, Trumbull Collection.

controversial. Colonial Americans were, at best, ambivalent about the stage and its usefulness to society, and theatrical performances had been actively discouraged in many British American provinces. Touring English theater companies had found friendly audiences in New York and in the southern colonies, but they generally had a chilly reception in Quaker Philadelphia. Theatrical performances were outlawed in New England, where descendants of the Puritans maintained the anti-theater traditions of their colonies' founders.

Even in locales where professional theater was legal and typically well-attended, however, it was sometimes controversial. For instance, in 1767–68, as colonists protested the Townshend Duties Act by boycotting British imports and struggled to make ends meet in a depressed economy, New Yorkers attacked the theater, which they now decried as a corrupting foreign luxury that gratified the rich while encouraging the poor to squander their money. Drawing on centuries of anti-theater rhetoric, critics also condemned the theater on moral grounds, characterizing both plays and actors as extravagant, debauched, and generally vicious influences in the wider community.

In 1774, the Continental Congress, calling for an end to extravagance and the renunciation of British imports to protest the Intolerable Acts that Parliament enacted to punish Massachusetts for the Boston Tea Party, made hostility to the theater the revolutionaries' official policy. Seeking to "encourage frugality, economy, and industry, and promote agriculture, arts and the manufactures of this country," Congress proscribed "plays" along with gambling, cock-fighting, horse-racing, expensive mourning clothes, and "every species of extravagance and dissipation."[8] Although soldiers and college students performed plays from time to time after 1774, professional theater virtually disappeared, except in cities occupied by British forces (most notably New York) during the revolutionary years.

When the war ended, theatrical performances resumed in some cities, but so did the controversy surrounding them. The pre-eminent touring English theater troupe of the colonial period, the American Company, returned to New York in 1785 after a decade of exile in Jamaica. A few new American theater troupes also were founded in the 1780s. The return of professional theater sparked major debates in cities such as New York, Philadelphia, and Charleston—where theater had been legal before the Revolution—as well as in Boston and other traditionally hostile New England communities.

In the 1780s, the theater's critics rehashed many old arguments, though the revolutionary achievement of independence and republican government infused their debates with a new political urgency. Opponents of the stage shrilly condemned the theater for promoting foreign (especially English) manners and ideas, emphasizing the London origins of both the actors and the plays they brought to American audiences. Citing Congress's ban on theater and loyalists' continued enjoyment of it, they associated the stage with counter-revolutionary political views. When critics asserted that the stage promoted bawdiness and that the costliness of tickets and demarcation of theater sections accentuated social inequality, they averred that the theater was not only immoral, but also anti-republican.

The theater's defenders also adapted their earlier contentions to the new political context. Like their colonial predecessors, they championed the didactic purposes of the stage, arguing that theatrical performances could teach morals and good manners to their audiences. Wholesome plays, they suggested, might even dramatize American history for those who would never read a history book and, through their characters, provide audiences with patriotic role models. To that end, most commentators conceded that the contents of theatrical performances should be regulated by the state to further these larger political and social purposes. Others took a more libertarian perspective, maintaining that Americans' revolutionary victory should secure, among other things, the freedom of citizens to choose the sort of entertainment they wanted.

By 1787, when the American Company performed *The Contrast* at New York's John Street Theatre, anti-theater forces had emerged triumphant everywhere except New York and Maryland. Although Tyler's play, a bawdy comedy of intrigue and near-seduction which drew heavily on contemporary English theater conventions, lent credence to some of the moral outrage vented in anti-theater circles, for the most part Tyler self-consciously used his play to spur thoughtful discourse on issues of political and cultural significance to post-revolutionary Americans. *The Contrast,* as affirmed in the play's prologue, was written by an American for his fellow-citizens. Its intent was to dramatize and scrutinize American manners, morals, and aspirations, as well as to ponder the supposed contrast between the United States and Europe in the post-revolutionary era. Tyler's purpose was as much didactic and political as it was artistic. "Should rigid critics reprobate our play," the prologue states, "At least the patriotic heart will say, / Glorious our fall, since in a noble cause. / The bold attempt alone demands applause." In March 1787, Major Royall Tyler traveled to New York as the emissary of Massachusetts governor James Bowdoin. Tyler's mission was to secure New York's assistance in apprehending any Shaysite rebels who crossed the border into New York to evade Massachusetts state authorities. In the preceding months, Tyler had served as aide-de-camp to General Benjamin Lincoln, the Continental Army veteran who commanded the state militia dispatched to suppress Shays's Rebellion.

Born in 1757 to a prosperous Boston family, Tyler graduated from Harvard in 1776. He served in the army briefly in 1778, but otherwise spent the war years studying law in and around Boston. Tyler was admitted to the bar in 1780. By 1787, he was a marginally successful lawyer, owner of a 108-acre farm in Braintree, Massachusetts, and the jilted suitor of the daughter of John and Abigail Adams. Tyler was well-edu-

Royall Tyler. This portrait, by an unknown artist, is the only known likeness of Royall Tyler. Only thirty years old when he wrote *The Contrast,* Tyler sat for this portrait later in life, after attaining prominence and prosperity as a judge and lawyer.

cated and well-read. Nevertheless, having lived his entire life in Massachusetts, where the stage was outlawed, he had probably never seen a professional theater production.

Tyler arrived in New York City on 12 March 1787, and his play, *The Contrast,* was advertised in the local press and performed at the John Street Theatre just five weeks later. In the intervening weeks, Tyler attended the theater in New York, where he saw both *The Poor Soldier,* a popular musical comedy by John O'Keeffe, and *The School for Scandal,* by the Irish playwright Richard Brinsley Sheridan, both productions that Tyler's characters would discuss in his own play. A well-received comedy of manners that poked fun at fashionable society and its pretensions, *The School for Scandal* may have inspired Tyler to address similar themes in an avowedly American context.

Shays's Rebellion and its aftermath provided the immediate context in which Tyler wrote *The Contrast* and also the framework within which his largely elite and urban audience would have interpreted the play. The comparison between rural virtue and plainness, on the one hand, and urban vice and sophistication, on the other, which was a common theme in English theater and fiction during this period, formed the core of Tyler's play. In the political and cultural discourse of post-revolutionary Americans, however, moralists and social critics often identified urban manners, duplicity, and vice with Europe, especially Britain, while idealizing virtue, simplicity, and transparency as characteristics of proper American republicans. Setting his play in an explicitly American context, New York in 1787, Tyler posed several timely questions. Most fundamentally, he asked how different, in truth, were post-revolutionary Americans from their European contemporaries—and how different should they be? Presenting his audience with characters representing a range of social types, Tyler also challenged them to consider which characters best corresponded to their own ideals and values.

In *The Contrast,* the characters in Tyler's main story of courtship, seduction, and marriage are "modern youths" of the rising post-revolutionary generation. They are stock figures, both in the real world and in the theatrical traditions of the era. Billy Dimple (whose name had been Van Dumpling before he toured Europe and became a disciple of Lord Chesterfield) is a foppish rake and sexual predator. Charlotte and Letitia are self-indulgent young women whose mindless pursuit of European-style fashion and pleasures make them susceptible to Dimple's ostentatious charms. Dimple, however, is engaged to marry Maria, the play's sentimental heroine, who reads novels and yearns to marry a virtuous man of sensibility but is nonetheless unwilling to disobey her father, the patriarchal Van Rough, who insists that she marry Dimple, who is heir to a large estate. The aptly named Colonel Henry Manly of Massachusetts, the play's hero and Charlotte's brother, is a patriot, soldier, and self-proclaimed man of integrity and virtue who models himself on—in his words—"our illustrious Washington."

The play's other main characters are young servants, who engage in their own comedic subplot of male-female relations while representing different lower-class social types. Dimple's servant, Jessamy, professes contentment with his social station but sees himself as his master's superior in both looks and manners. A more crude and misogynistic parody of his master, Jessamy studies and quotes Chesterfield, acts worldly, and aims to seduce unsuspecting women. The good, earnest, rustic Jonathan, whom literary scholars regard as "a significant creation of the Yankee type,"[9] describes himself not as a "servant" but as Manly's "waiter." Jonathan, who sees his servitude as temporary, is the son of a New England farmer. He asserts that he is his master's equal, yet he defers to Manly's political opinions, at least in the case of Shays's Rebellion. Jenny, the prize sought both by Jessamy and (more reluctantly) by Jonathan, considers herself a "lady," but her status as a servant leaves her unprotected and thus vulnerable to male advances, which she—unlike her genteel elite counterparts—must fend off herself.

Other lesser characters, most of whom never appear on stage, complete Tyler's portrait of contemporary New York society. Charlotte's repetition of gossip she heard from her "aunt Wyerly's Hannah," an enslaved woman, suggests a casual acceptance of both slavery and interaction with black servants among New York's elite. Other unnamed servants—presumably white—appear on stage, forming part of the social landscape of genteel New Yorkers in the 1780s. At the other end of the social scale, are the milliner, Mrs. Catgut, and her clients, Sally Slender, Miss Blouze, and Miss Wasp, whose names denote not only their respective appearances but also the propensity of fashionable society to judge individuals solely by their external qualities. Jonathan's female acquaintances in rural New England, by contrast, included women with names like Tabitha Wymen and Jemima Cawley.

The Contrast begins with a long prologue in which the author emphasizes that both his characters and their setting are American, though his play will tell the stories of those young adults who ape European manners and dress and have abandoned the "homespun habits" of the revolutionary generation. The play's prologue strikes an ambivalent note. Admitting that it might be "strange" for Americans to reject their "native worth" and thereby "check the progress of our rising fame," as countless critics of luxury and foreign influence had observed, the author suggests that one who imitates ideals of any sort "aspires to nobler heights, and points the way" for others. What models, then, should Americans find worthy of emulation? The five acts of *The Contrast* employ humor and melodrama in an attempt to answer that timely but vexing question.

The play opens with Charlotte and Letitia discussing fashion, flirting, and the impending marriage of Billy Dimple, whom they both admire, to Maria Van Rough. Years earlier, the youngsters' fathers had arranged the financially advantageous match. In the ensuing years of their betrothal, however, a European tour transformed William Van Dumpling into the anglicized fop Billy Dimple, while novel-reading led Maria to admire men of virtue and sensibility. The sentimental Maria now considers the debauched Billy "unmanly," but she feels duty-bound to obey her father, who insists on her wedding the heir to Dumpling Manor. For their part, Charlotte and Letitia aver that, when it comes to marriage, considerations of wealth and status should be paramount.

In Act II, Tyler introduces his hero, Colonel Henry Manly, who appears, dressed in his old Continental Army uniform, at the elegant New York house where his sister, Charlotte, resides with their uncle. Manly, who recently participated in the suppression of Shays's Rebellion, has come to New York on business. He scorns the frivolity of urban polite society. Charlotte describes her brother as grave, old-fashioned, moralistic, and ungallant—and, indeed, he is. But Tyler's audience would have recognized this patriotic Yankee landowner who cared for his aging parents, cherished his ties to fellow-soldiers, and spurned luxury and artifice as the personification of idealized republican values.

Manly's "waiter," Jonathan, shares his employer's loyalty to family and country, as well as his plain manners. The first meeting between the unsophisticated Jonathan and the Chesterfield-quoting, French–phrase-dropping Jessamy foreshadows the contrast between Manly and Dimple. Jonathan, who has never been to the city and knows no formal rules of etiquette, expects to wed his "true-love," whose dowry consists of twenty rocky acres, a Bible, and a cow—an arrangement that seems to strike a happy balance between heartfelt emotion and common-sense practicality. Jessamy, however, convinces Jonathan that he can do much better by wooing Maria's servant, Jenny. Pretending to instruct Jonathan in the Chesterfieldian method of seduction, Jessamy instead advises him to act in ways that are guaranteed to offend her. Having established the "contrast . . . between the blundering Jonathan and the courtly and accomplished Jessamy," the latter gleefully expects to have an easier time seducing Jenny himself.

Act III opens with the first appearance of Billy Dimple and establishes the contrast between Dimple and Manly, who stand at opposite ends of the spectrum of eighteenth-century elite masculine types. Billy is

Plan of the City of New York, 1789. Tyler set his play in New York, the second largest city in America, which had a population of roughly 30,000, the vast majority of whom lived in Lower Manhattan, south of present-day Houston Street. The public promenade, where Manly and Dimple met, is in Battery Park at the island's southern tip. The John Street Theatre, where *The Contrast* was first performed, was located near Broadway, south of the open triangle (now City Hall Park). Library of Congress.

a rake who changed his name from "Dumpling" (a plain but substantial source of sustenance) to "Dimple" (an ornamental but empty space). Significantly, when the audience gets its first glimpse of Billy Dimple, he is primping and reading aloud from Chesterfield's instructions on how to flatter and manipulate women. Having fallen deeply into debt as a result of his profligate habits, Dimple is scheming to alienate Maria so that he can marry the wealthy Letitia, though he prefers the beautiful Charlotte, whom he hopes to seduce and keep as his mistress.

Colonel Henry Manly, by contrast, is a man of integrity and sensibility. Manly and Dimple first encounter each other on the Mall, the tree-lined promenade in lower Manhattan where fashionable people strolled, displayed themselves, and scrutinized others. As Dimple approaches Manly, the latter soliloquizes at length about the dangers of luxury, especially in republics. Dimple tries to ingratiate himself with the colonel by professing admiration for brave soldiers, but he offends Manly when he offers to introduce him to innocent girls "who will listen to your soft things with pleasure." In contrast to Dimple's conceptions of women as disposable sexual toys or stepping stones to upward mobility, Manly argues that the virtues of the sexes are complementary and that men and women should be companions to each other. Dimple feigns agreement and then regretfully discovers that Charlotte, his intended mistress, is Manly's sister.

In Act IV, Manly and Maria finally meet, and they are predictably taken with each other. While Manly sees in Maria a virtuous companion, she admires him as a man who, unlike Dimple, speaks the "language of sentiment." Sadly, Maria still believes that she is obliged to obey her father by marrying Dimple, and Manly, for his part, concurs. Meanwhile, unbeknownst to them, Maria's father, Van Rough, learns of Dimple's debts.

Revelations about Dimple's financial troubles, as well as his dastardly designs on Charlotte and Letitia, lead to the play's unsurprisingly happy ending in Act V. As Dimple attempts to seduce Charlotte, who resists his advances, Manly enters to defend his sister's honor. Letitia, who overhears the meeting between Charlotte and Manly, also rejects the duplicitous Dimple, who tries to reconcile with Maria, only to be repulsed by the outraged Van Rough. Dimple's disgrace leaves Charlotte and Letitia chastened, penitent, and seemingly committed to moral reformation. With Van Rough's permission, Maria and Manly are free to marry. Virtue, integrity, and honor, the characters agree, are the true guarantors of happiness and love.

Tyler's resolution of Jonathan's story is less explicit. Jenny, indeed, rejects the hapless Jonathan, who, on Jessamy's advice, awkwardly tries to seduce the young woman. Jessamy gives Jonathan a second etiquette lesson which, like the first, he carefully calculates to make Jonathan's conduct absurd and boorishly offensive. Jessamy attempts to transform the rustic Jonathan into a clumsy caricature of Chesterfieldian artifice, but Jonathan ultimately rejects his tutelage. A second meeting between Jonathan and Jenny does not occur. The play's final scene finds Jonathan witnessing the altercation between Manly and Dimple and springing to his master's defense. This conclusion implies that Jonathan's virtue survived its encounter with Jessamy's vices and that he will return to Massachusetts, marry his sweetheart, and defer to the leadership of men like Manly.

At the play's end, by contrast, neither Dimple nor Jessamy shows any prospect of reform. Dimple storms off stage angrily, insisting that having "read Chesterfield and received the polish of Europe" make him different from (and, in his view, superior to) Manly. Dimple will probably go elsewhere to prey on unsuspecting women and their families; assuming that Dimple can pay his wages, Jessamy will go with him. Here, Tyler's message is twofold. On the one hand, rakes and confidence men are part of the social landscape in America, perhaps even more than elsewhere. On the other hand, *The Contrast* exposes and discredits such evildoers and shows that virtue and integrity can thwart their efforts. In this respect, Tyler's message is similar to that of many contemporary sentimental novels.

Nevertheless, Tyler wrote *The Contrast* to address other timely public issues by pondering the supposed differences between American virtue and European vice and raising two broadly related questions about the future of manners, morals, and authority in post-revolutionary America. First, Tyler allows the audience to scrutinize his characters before considering whether idealized republican virtue, as described by contemporary moralists and social critics, was attainable or even desirable now that the war was over. Second, and more generally, *The Contrast* asks what the values and culture of post-revolutionary Americans ought to be—and offers a prescription for the future that seeks to reconcile revolutionary republican ideals with the postwar fears of conservative elites.

In response to those who would celebrate or cultivate a uniquely American civic virtue, Tyler suggests that even demonstrably virtuous Americans could not meet the lofty standards of republican ideologues. Tyler's heroes, though admirable, are at best flawed characters. Patriotic and hard-working, Jonathan is also ill-informed and easily manipulated and deceived. Indeed, when he first meets Jessamy, Jonathan thinks that the loquacious servant looks "so topping" that he must be a member of Congress. Clearly, Tyler's representative common man, Jonathan, lacks the discernment contemporaries associated with idealized republican citizenship. Similarly, the novel-reading Maria, though undeniably virtuous and patriotic, is no flawless exemplar of republican womanhood. Maria's wedding clothes are not homespun, but "delicate white satin" that—in Charlotte's words—"would shew her clear skin and dark hair to the greatest advantage." Although her father called her "Mary," Tyler's heroine made another concession to European-style gentility by adopting the more fashionable name "Maria."

In Colonel Henry Manly, Tyler created a character who epitomized republican ideals, but many contemporaries would have regarded Manly, too, as an imperfect prototype for American manhood in the post-revolutionary years. The moralistic, pedantic, and somewhat anti-social Manly is a caricature of republican virtue. Tyler probably expected audiences to snicker at the style and length of his recurring soliloquies, if not at their content. (The revolutionary era was an age of oratory, but Manly was no Patrick Henry.) Audiences also may have shared Charlotte's disapproval of her brother's insistence on wearing his tattered military uniform four years after the war was over. Americans revered George Washington for resigning his military commission in 1783, after which he typically wore civilian clothes. "The greatest act of [Washington's] life, the one that gave him his greatest fame," a leading historian has observed, "was his resignation as commander in chief of the American forces."[10] A man of notoriously few words, unlike Colonel Manly, Washington was America's hero in part because he could both embody and transcend the achievements of the revolutionary years.

Tyler's point was not that Manly and Maria—or for that matter Jonathan—were bad, because clearly they were not. The patriotism, honesty, and moderation of these characters, and the fact that their stories end happily, suggest that Tyler was optimistic about the ability of Americans like them to preserve the republic that the Revolution had established. At the same time, by making his representative Americans imperfect, Tyler implicitly agreed with contemporary proponents of a stronger central government, who contended that carefully constructed political institutions could promote the general welfare by shielding government from the passions of the people. As James Madison, chief author of and leading advocate for the U.S. Constitution, wrote in 1788, "What is government itself, but the greatest of all reflections on human nature? If men were angels, no government would be necessary."[11]

Tyler's social criticism is limited and generally moderate, even on the central issues of luxury and gentility. *The Contrast* features a spectrum of characters. At one extreme, is the pastoral, innocent, and unrefined Jonathan. At the other, are Dimple, Charlotte, Letitia, and Jessamy, whose slavish pursuit of European luxuries leaves them incapable of patriotism, friendship, piety, or love. Manly and Maria, who occupy the middle of Tyler's continuum, combine Jonathan's moral virtue with a moderate and sensitive version of genteel refinement. A combination of sensibility, politeness, and personal responsibility (toward both superi-

George Washington, by Jean-Antoine Houdon, 1785–1792. This slightly larger-than-life-sized sculpture, which graces the Virginia Capitol in Richmond, captured Washington at his most heroic, from the perspective of his contemporaries. A uniformed Washington exchanges his sword and military cape for the walking stick and plow of a gentleman farmer. These symbols of civilian life appear in Washington's right hand and behind him, respectively. Courtesy of the Library of Virginia.

ors and dependents) makes them Tyler's most admirable, if still imperfect, characters.

Tyler uses language and grammar, along with clothing, as cultural markers to delineate both the moral stances of his characters and their social ranks. The clear and measured pronouncements of Manly and Maria indicate their moral superiority over Dimple and his circle, whose affected and intemperate speech is often profane and peppered with foreign words, while Jonathan's use of rustic dialect and poor grammar mark him as Manly and Maria's social inferior. Similarly, the elaborate clothing of Dimple, Charlotte, and Letitia is emblematic of self-indulgence and artifice, while Jessamy's pretensions to fashion both mirror and enable his duplicitous efforts to corrupt Jenny and Jonathan. In "polite circles," moreover, clothing blurs gender differences—a grave prospect for a society that deems the sexes complementary—as women and men alike don frills and silks to be "dressy" and "delicate." In the context of such artifice and uncertainty, patriotic Manly, soberly genteel Maria, and plebeian Jonathan are transparent. Their attire signifies both their moral and social attributes.

What, then, was Tyler's prescription for post-revolutionary Americans? How did *The Contrast* address the basic questions involving morality, authority, and national identity which Americans debated in the post-revolutionary years?

In *The Contrast,* Tyler tacitly accepted existing social and political inequalities. Although a decade later he would publish an anti-slavery novel, *The Algerine Captive,* in 1787 he did not criticize slavery in New York, though it recently had been abolished in his own home state. Nor did *The Contrast* include a critique of white servitude in America. Both Jonathan and Jessamy were subservient to and dependent on their masters, though they were loath to admit it; Tyler ridicules Jessamy's outlandish assertions of gentility and gently mocks Jonathan's pretensions to equality. While Jessamy suffers morally (and possibly economically) as a result of his ties to the unscrupulous Dimple, Tyler implies that Jonathan's association with Manly benefits him, as it does society generally.

Tyler's portrayal of the relationship between Manly and Jonathan supports the contention, shared by all opponents of Shays's Rebellion and most future proponents of the U.S. Constitution, that a "natural aristocracy" of virtuous and enlightened men was best-suited to govern the American republic. Like many non-elite farmers, Jonathan initially believed "the sturgeons [insurgents] were right," but, as he confided to Jessamy, Manly convinced his father, brother, and ultimately Jonathan himself that Shays's Rebellion threatened to undermine the achievements of the Revolution in which they all had shared. Tyler may have modeled this episode on his own experience during Shays's Rebellion, when, on capturing a group of rebels, he used magnanimity and eloquence to affect "the instant conversion of the whole band into good citizens."[12] In both instances, from the perspective of those who feared popular rule, the influence of a wise and disinterested leader quelled the disorder and conflict that endangered the survival of the republic.

So, too, did Tyler defend existing gender hierarchies. One might expect the crass and unsentimental Van Rough, who affectionately calls Maria his "little baggage," to regard his daughter as a negotiable commodity. Yet, Manly, a man of feeling and integrity, also respects the legal and social conventions that made females a species of property. On learning that Maria was betrothed to the despicable Billy Dimple, Manly's main concern was to preserve his own honor. He worried that by conversing with Maria, a betrothed woman, he was "basely invading the rights of another." Manly also agreed that Van Rough had the authority to decide his daughter's destiny, even if that led to her marrying a vicious man she did not love.

Without rejecting patriarchy, however, *The Contrast* ultimately suggests that the companionate marriage ideal was the most compatible with American republican values. In Tyler's play, the characters who favor mercenary or otherwise loveless matches are the backward-looking Van Rough, the unsympathetic Dimple, and the foolish Charlotte. Because Van Rough is old, Dimple is ostracized, and Charlotte renounces her coquettish ways, these characters and their ideals will not shape the future. Manly and Maria, Tyler's more sympathetic characters, view marriage as source of companionship and love.

The betrothal of Manly and Maria signifies both the triumph of the companionate ideal and the preservation of order and social hierarchy. Maria and Manly ask and receive Van Rough's permission to marry. Van Rough already has inquired around town about Manly's property and prospects, and the colonel, for his part, offers to furnish his prospective father-in-law with references who will vouch for him. Though Manly might be a stranger to Van Rough, the old man thus follows the traditional practice of using personal contacts to evaluate his daughter's suitor, and Manly condones those traditional practices. Finally, because Manly is a landowner and Maria is a merchant's daughter, their union solidifies, rather than challenges, the existing social hierarchy. Although the Van Roughs are wealthier than Manly, the colonel has more public stature. At least in terms of the social status of their respective families, theirs will be a marriage of equals.

In the context of the impending Federal Convention in Philadelphia, the union of Manly and Maria also forged bonds necessary for the creation of a national ruling elite. Their marriage joined Manly's virtuous patriotism to the economic power of the seemingly apolitical Van Rough. In addition, it represented an alliance of landed and commercial interests, as well as a bridging of the long-standing ethnic divide between Yankee New Englanders and New York Dutch. Tyler envisioned a republican elite that encompassed men of different regions, interests, and outlooks. Together, such men would constitute a natural aristocracy that honored the legacy of the Revolution but moved forward to embrace the task of nation-building, bringing order, prosperity, and stability to the post-revolutionary republican world.

Contemporary response to *The Contrast* was overwhelmingly positive. In New York and elsewhere, cultural nationalists applauded the play as evidence of American artistic achievement. *The Contrast,* explained one representative reviewer, was "an additional specimen in proof that these new climes are particularly favorable to the cultivation of arts and sciences." Tyler followed up his initial success with another offering, a comic opera entitled *May Day in Town,* which debuted at the John Street Theatre on 19 May 1787. According to one contemporary observer, this now mostly lost piece "has plott & incident and is as good as several of the English farces . . . [but] has however not succeeded well, owing I believe to the Author's making his principal character a scold."[13] Royall Tyler's foray into the world of theater brought him fame, if not wealth.

Not long after the premiere of this second play, Tyler returned home to Massachusetts. By 1790, he had married and settled in Vermont, where he resumed his legal practice. A moderate Federalist in a largely rural Republican state, Tyler nonetheless became both successful and highly regarded as a justice of the state Supreme Court, ultimately assuming the rank of chief justice. Tyler taught law at the University of Vermont and published his two-volume *Reports of Cases Argued and Determined in the Supreme Court of Judicature of the State of Vermont* in 1809 and 1810. He also continued to write fiction and essays. After 1813, however, Tyler's life took a turn for the worse as he lost his judgeship and developed a form of cancer in his face which eventually left him blind and unable to work. He died in poverty in Vermont in August 1826.

Tyler's best-known work, *The Contrast,* was an important contribution in a pivotal period in American history. The play's popularity suggests that it struck a responsive chord among contemporary audiences. In what was a notably successful run for the times, *The Contrast* was performed four times at the John Street Theatre in 1787. In 1789, shortly after George Washington assumed the presidency in New York, the nation's first capital under the new constitution, Tyler's play was restaged there. Both Baltimore and Philadelphia also hosted performances of *The Contrast* between 1788 and 1790. When Thomas Wignell, the actor who played the role of Jonathan, sought financial support to fund the publication of Tyler's play in book form, he found 371 subscribers, some of whom purchased multiple copies. When *The Contrast* appeared in print for the first time in 1790, President Washington himself headed the published list of subscribers. Timely themes and a comforting political message accounted for the continuing appeal of Tyler's play, which was staged in several American cities during the 1790s.

Although professional theater itself was increasingly accepted throughout the United States after 1800, nineteenth-century theater companies rarely performed *The Contrast.* Theater historians and critics still credited Tyler's play as "the commencement of the American drama as united with the American theatre."[14] *The Contrast* was, in other words, an American first. At the same time, however, nineteenth-century commentators attributed the decline in the play's popularity to its various alleged shortcomings and changing tastes in drama and literature. In fact, pieces written by or adapted from British playwrights dominated professional theater in the United States well into the nineteenth century.

A more compelling explanation for the diminished appeal of *The Contrast* was the fact that Tyler's play was first and foremost a didactic response to the political and cultural issues of the late 1780s. The questions Tyler raised about appropriate morals, manners, and social relations for American republicans were answered, at least for the time being, in the decade or so after 1787. When Americans returned to these issues, as they would in the ensuing centuries, Tyler's prescriptions, born of the uncertainties of the post-revolutionary years, would be anachronistic and quaintly irrelevant.

In other respects, however, Tyler's play, though no longer a staple of the American stage, remains both amusing and relevant. In April 2006, 219 years to the day after its first performance, *The Contrast* opened for a five-week revival at a New York City theater. The reviews were generally positive.[15] Critics noted the class and ethic diversity of Tyler's characters—an enduring hallmark of American life—as well as the characters' still timely disagreement over the relative merits of image and reality, form and content. "*The Contrast* is an important piece of American theatrical history," one critic asserted, adding that it also "remains a charming and thoroughly enjoyable American play" more than two centuries after it received the endorsement of George Washington.

NOTES

1. George Washington to James Madison, 5 Nov. 1786, in John C. Fitzpatrick, ed., *The Writings of George Washington*, 39 vols. (Washington: U.S. Government Printing Office, 1931–44), 29:51. See also Washington to John Jay, 1 Aug. 1786, in ibid., 28:501–4.

2. George R. Minot, *The History of the Insurrection in Massachusetts in 1786 and of the Rebellion Consequent Thereon* (Worcester, Mass.: Isaiah Thomas, 1788), 82–83.

3. "The Influence of the Female Sex on the Enjoyments of Social Life," *Columbian Magazine*, 4 (1790): 154.

4. See especially Jay Fliegelman, *Prodigals and Pilgrims: The American Revolution against Patriarchal Authority, 1750–1800* (Cambridge, Eng.: Cambridge University Press, 1982).

5. Susanna Haswell Rowson, *Charlotte Temple*, ed. Cathy N. Davidson (New York: Oxford University Press, 1986), 5.

6. George Washington to Mathew Carey, [25 June 1788], quoted in Kenneth Silverman, *A Cultural History of the American Revolution* (New York: Crowell, 1976), 487; "Preface," *Columbian Magazine*, 1 (1786): 1.

7. Philip Freneau and Hugh Henry Brackenridge, "A Poem, on the Rising Glory of America," in Eve Kornfeld, *Creating an American Culture: A Brief History with Documents* (New York: Bedford/St. Martin's, 2001), 87.

8. Continental Association, 20 Oct. 1774, in *Journals of the Continental Congress, 1774–1789*, ed. Worthington C. Ford et al., (Washington, D.C.: Government Printing Office, 1904–37), 1: 78.

9. Donald T. Siebert, Jr., "Royall Tyler's 'Bold Experiment': *The Contrast* and the English Comedy of Manners," *Early American Literature*, 13 (1978): 3.

10. Gordon S. Wood, *The Radicalism of the American Revolution* (New York: Alfred A. Knopf, 1992), 205.

11. [James Madison], *The Federalist*, Number 51, [6 Feb. 1788], in Robert A. Rutland, et al., eds., *The Papers of James Madison* (Chicago: University of Chicago Press, 1962–), 10: 477.

12. Thomas Pickman Tyler, "Memoir of Royall Tyler," typescript, Vermont Historical Society, n.d., quoted in Richard S. Pressman, "Class Positioning and Shays' Rebellion: Resolving the Contradictions of *The Contrast*," *Early American Literature*, 21 (1986): 92.

13. *Pennsylvania Herald*, 13 Nov. 1787, quoted in Silverman, *Cultural History of the American Revolution*, 562; William Grayson to James Madison, 24 May 1787, in Rutland, et al., eds., *Papers of James Madison*, 9:418.

14. William Dunlap, *A History of the American Theatre, from Its Origins to 1832*, ed. Tice L. Miller (1832; Urbana: University of Illinois Press, 2005), 75.

15. See, for instance, Loren Noveck, "The Contrast," 16 Apr. 2006, at http://www.nytheatre.com/nytheatre/archweb/arch2006_19.htm#455 [accessed 31 May 2006]; Alexis Soloski, "Dearth of a Nation," *The Village Voice*, 25 Apr. 2006, at http://www.villagevoice.com/theater/0617,soloski,73000,11.html [accessed 31 May 2006].

2

The Contrast by Royall Tyler

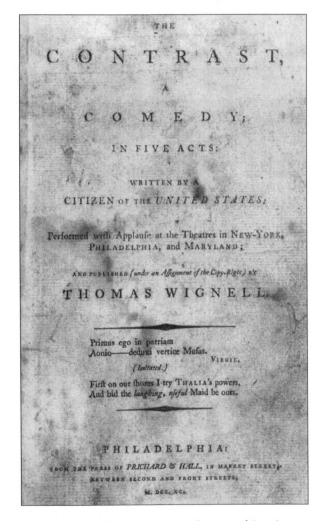

Title page from *The Contrast*, 1790. Courtesy of American Antiquarian Society.

ADVERTISEMENT.

The Subscribers (to whom the Editor thankfully professes his obligations) may reasonably expect an apology for the delay which has attended the appearance of *The Contrast;* but, as the true cause cannot be declared without leading to a discussion, which the Editor wishes to avoid, he hopes that the care and expense which have been bestowed upon this work will be accepted, without further scrutiny, as an atonement for his seeming negligence.

In justice to the Author, however, it may be proper to observe that this Comedy has many claims to the public indulgence, independent of its intrinsic merits: It is the first essay of American genius in a difficult species of composition; it was written by one who never critically studied the rules of drama, and, indeed, had seen but few of the exhibitions of the stage; it was undertaken and finished in the course of three weeks; and the profits from one night's performance were appropriated to the benefit of the sufferers by the fire at *Boston.*

These considerations will, therefore, it is hoped, supply in the closet the advantages that are derived from representation, and dispose the reader to join in the applause which has been bestowed on this Comedy by numerous and judicious audiences, in the Theatres of *Philadelphia, New-York,* and *Maryland.*

As a Just Acknowledgement of the Liberal Exertions
By which the *Stage* has been Rescued from
An Ignominious Proscription,

The Contrast

(Being the First Essay of *American* Genius in the Dramatic Art)

is Most Respectfully Dedicated
to
The President and Members of the
Dramatic Association,

By
Their Most Obliged
And
Most Grateful Servant,

Thomas Wignell

Philadelphia
1 January 1790

PROLOGUE

Written by a Young Gentleman of New-York, and Spoken by Mr. Wignell.

Exult, each patriot heart!—this night is shewn
A piece, which we may fairly call our own;
Where the proud titles of "My Lord! Your Grace!"
To humble Mr. and plain Sir give place.
Our Author pictures not from foreign climes
The fashions or the follies of the times;
But has confin'd the subject of his work
To the gay scenes—the circles of New-York.
On native themes his Muse displays her pow'rs;
If ours the faults, the virtues too are ours.
Why should our thoughts to distant countries roam,
When each refinement may be found at home?
Who travels now to ape the rich or great,
To deck an equipage and roll in state;
To court the graces, or to dance with ease,
Or by hypocrisy to strive to please?
Our free-born ancestors such arts despis'd;
Genuine sincerity alone they priz'd;
Their minds, with honest emulation fir'd;
To solid good—not ornament—aspir'd;
Or, if ambition rous'd a bolder flame,
Stern virtue throve, where indolence was shame.

But modern youths, with imitative sense,
Deem taste in dress the proof of excellence;
And spurn the meanness of your homespun arts,
Since homespun habits would obscure their parts;
Whilst all, which aims at splendour and parade,
Must come from Europe, and be ready made.
Strange! we should thus our native worth disclaim,
And check the progress of our rising fame.

Yet one, *whilst imitation bears the sway,*
Aspires to nobler heights, and points the way.

Be rous'd, my friends! his bold example view;
Let your own Bards be proud to copy you!
Should rigid critics reprobate our play,
At least the patriotic heart will say,
"Glorious our fall, since in a noble cause.
The bold *attempt alone demands applause."*
Still may the wisdom of the Comic Muse
Exalt your merits, or your faults accuse.
But think not, 'tis her aim to be severe;—
We all are mortals, and as mortals err.
If candour pleases, we are truly blest;
Vice trembles, when compell'd to stand confess'd.
Let not light Censure on your faults offend,
Which aims not to expose them, but amend.
Thus does our Author to your candour trust;
Conscious, the free *are generous, as just.*

CHARACTERS.

	New-York.	Maryland.
Col. Manly,	Mr *Henry.*	Mr *Hallam.*
Dimple,	Mr *Hallam.*	Mr *Harper.*
Van Rough	Mr *Morris.*	Mr *Morris.*
Jessamy,	Mr *Harper.*	Mr *Biddle.*
Jonathan,	Mr *Wignell.*	Mr *Wignell.*
Charlotte,	Mrs *Morris.*	Mrs *Morris.*
Maria,	Mrs *Harper.*	Mrs *Harper.*
Letitia,	Mrs *Kenna.*	Mrs *Williamson.*
Jenny,	Miss *Tuke.*	Miss *W. Tuke.*
Servants.		

Scene, *New-York.*

The Contrast

Act I.

SCENE I.

Scene, an Apartment at CHARLOTTE's.
CHARLOTTE *and* LETITIA *discovered.*

LETITIA: And so, Charlotte, you really think the pocket-hoop[1] unbecoming.

CHARLOTTE: No, I don't say so. It may be very becoming to saunter round the house of a rainy day; to visit my grand-mamma, or to go to Quakers' meeting: but to swim in a minuet, with the eyes of fifty well-dressed beaux upon me, to trip it in the Mall, or walk on the battery, give me the luxurious, jaunty, flowing, bell-hoop. It would have delighted you to have seen me the last evening, my charming girl! I was dangling o'er the battery with Billy Dimple; a knot of young fellows were upon the platform; as I passed them I faultered with one of the most bewitching false steps you ever saw, and then recovered myself with such a pretty confusion, flirting my hoop to discover a jet black shoe and brilliant buckle. Gad! how my little heart thrilled to hear the confused raptures of—"*Demme,*[2] *Jack, what a delicate foot!*" "*Ha! General, what a well-turned—*"

LETITIA: Fie! fie! Charlotte [*stopping her mouth*], I protest you are quite a libertine.

CHARLOTTE: Why, my dear little prude, are we not all such libertines? Do you think, when I sat tortured two hours under the hands of my friseur,[3] and an hour more at my toilet, that I had any thoughts of my aunt Susan, or my cousin Betsey? though they are both allowed to be critical judges of dress.

---

[1] Pocket-hoops, fashionable after 1750, extended skirts beyond the hips at either side to create a wide silhouette from the waist down. The bell-hoop, which created a more streamlined skirt, eventually supplanted the pocket-hoop in popularity.

[2] Demme: damn.

[3] Friseur: hairdresser.

LETITIA: Why, who should we dress to please, but those who are judges of its merit?

CHARLOTTE: Why, a creature who does not know *Buffon*[4] from *Soufleè* —Man!—my Letitia—Man! for whom we dress, walk, dance, talk, lisp, languish, and smile. Does not the grave Spectator[5] assure us that even our much bepraised diffidence, modesty, and blushes are all directed to make ourselves good wives and mothers as fast as we can? Why, I'll undertake with one flirt of this hoop to bring more beaux to my feet in one week than the grave Maria, and her sentimental circle, can do, by sighing sentiment till their hairs are grey.

LETITIA: Well, I won't argue with you; you always out-talk me; let us change the subject. I hear that Mr. Dimple and Maria are soon to be married.

CHARLOTTE: You hear true. I was consulted in the choice of the wedding clothes. She is to be married in a delicate white sattin, and has a monstrous pretty brocaded lutestring[6] for the second day. It would have done you good to have seen with what an affected indifference the dear sentimentalist turned over a thousand pretty things, just as if her heart did not palpitate with her approaching happiness, and at last made her choice and arranged her dress with such apathy as if she did not know that plain white sattin and a simple blond lace would shew her clear skin and dark hair to the greatest advantage.

LETITIA: But they say her indifference to dress, and even to the gentleman himself, is not entirely affected.

CHARLOTTE: How?

LETITIA: It is whispered that if Maria gives her hand to Mr. Dimple, it will be without her heart.

CHARLOTTE: Though the giving the heart is one of the last of all laughable considerations in the marriage of a girl of spirit, yet I should like to hear what antiquated notions the dear little piece of old-fashioned prudery has got in her head.

LETITIA: Why, you know that old Mr. John-Richard-Robert-Jacob-

---

[4] Georges-Louis LeClerc, Comte de Buffon (1707–1788), was an important French naturalist who argued, among other things, that Old World species were larger than—and therefore superior to—those of the Americas.

[5] The *Spectator* essays (1711–1714), by Joseph Addison and Richard Steele, were published in London and widely read in America. Addison and Steele promoted civility, respected women's moral influence, and were generally critical of luxury and vice.

[6] Lutestring: a glossy silk fabric.

Isaac-Abraham-Cornelius Van Dumpling, Billy Dimple's father (for he has thought fit to soften his name, as well as manners, during his English tour), was the most intimate friend of Maria's father. The old folks, about a year before Mr. Van Dumpling's death, proposed this match: the young folks were accordingly introduced, and told they must love one another. Billy was then a good-natured, decent-dressing young fellow, with a little dash of the coxcomb, such as our young fellows of fortune usually have. At this time, I really believe she thought she loved him; and had they been married, I doubt not they might have jogged on, to the end of the chapter, a good kind of a sing-song lack-a-daysaical life, as other honest married folks do.

CHARLOTTE: Why did they not then marry?

LETITIA: Upon the death of his father, Billy went to England to see the world and rub off a little of the patroon rust. During his absence, Maria, like a good girl, to keep herself constant to her *nown true-love,* avoided company, and betook herself, for her amusement, to her books, and her dear Billy's letters. But, alas! how many ways has the mischievous demon of inconstancy of stealing into a woman's heart! Her love was destroyed by the very means she took to support it.

CHARLOTTE: How?—Oh! I have it—some likely young beau found the way to her study.

LETITIA: Be patient, Charlotte; your head so runs upon beaux. Why, she read Sir Charles Grandison, Clarissa Harlow, Shenstone, and the Sentimental Journey;[7] and between whiles, as I said, Billy's letters. But, as her taste improved, her love declined. The contrast was so striking betwixt the good sense of her books and the flimsiness of her love-letters, that she discovered she had unthinkingly engaged her hand without her heart; and then the whole transaction, managed by the old folks, now appeared so unsentimental, and looked so like bargaining for a bale of goods, that she found she ought to have rejected, according to every rule of romance, even the man of her choice, if imposed upon her in that manner. Clary Harlow would have scorned such a match.

CHARLOTTE: Well, how was it on Mr. Dimple's return? Did he meet a more favourable reception than his letters?

---

[7] *Clarissa* (1748) and *Sir Charles Grandison* (1753) were popular sentimental novels by the English writer Samuel Richardson. *Sentimental Journey* (1768) was written by Laurence Sterne, an Irish novelist. William Shenstone was an English novelist and poet.

LETITIA: Much the same. She spoke of him with respect abroad, and with contempt in her closet. She watched his conduct and conversation, and found that he had by travelling acquired the wickedness of Lovelace without his wit, and the politeness of Sir Charles Grandison without his generosity. The ruddy youth, who washed his face at the cistern every morning, and swore and looked eternal love and constancy, was now metamorphosed into a flippant, palid, polite beau, who devotes the morning to his toilet, reads a few pages of Chesterfield's letters, and then minces out, to put the infamous principles in practice upon every woman he meets.

CHARLOTTE: But, if she is so apt at conjuring up these sentimental bugbears, why does she not discard him at once?

LETITIA: Why, she thinks her word too sacred to be trifled with. Besides, her father, who has a great respect for the memory of his deceased friend, is ever telling her how he shall renew his years in their union, and repeating the dying injunctions of old Van Dumpling.

CHARLOTTE: A mighty pretty story! And so you would make me believe that the sensible Maria would give up Dumpling manor, and the all-accomplished Dimple as a husband, for the absurd, ridiculous reason, forsooth, because she despises and abhors him. Just as if a lady could not be privileged to spend a man's fortune, ride in his carriage, be called after his name, and call him her *nown dear lovee* when she wants money, without loving and respecting the great he-creature. Oh! my dear girl, you are a monstrous prude.

LETITIA: I don't say what I would do; I only intimate how I suppose she wishes to act.

CHARLOTTE: No, no, no! A fig for sentiment. If she breaks, or wishes to break, with Mr. Dimple, depend upon it, she has some other man in her eye. A woman rarely discards one lover until she is sure of another. [*Aside, and rings a bell.*] Letitia little thinks what a clue I have to Dimple's conduct. The generous man submits to render himself disgusting to Maria, in order that she may leave him at liberty to address me. I must change the subject.

Enter SERVANT.

Frank, order the horses to—Talking of marriage, did you hear that Sally Bloomsbury is going to be married next week to Mr. Indigo, the rich Carolinian?

LETITIA: Sally Bloomsbury married!—why, she is not yet in her teens.

CHARLOTTE: I do not know how that is, but you may depend upon it, 'tis a done affair. I have it from the best authority. There is my aunt Wyerly's Hannah. You know Hannah; though a black, she is a wench that was never caught in a lie in her life. Now, Hannah has a brother who courts Sarah, Mrs. Catgut the milliner's girl, and she told Hannah's brother, and Hannah, who, as I said before, is a girl of undoubted veracity, told it directly to me, that Mrs. Catgut was making a new cap for Miss Bloomsbury, which, as it was very dressy, it is very probable is designed for a wedding cap. Now, as she is to be married, who can it be to but to Mr. Indigo? Why, there is no other gentleman that visits at her papa's.

LETITIA: Say not a word more, Charlotte. Your intelligence is so direct and well grounded, it is almost a pity that it is not a piece of scandal.

CHARLOTTE: Oh! I am the pink of prudence. Though I cannot charge myself with ever having discredited a tea-party by my silence, yet I take care never to report any thing of my acquaintance, especially if it is to their credit,—*discredit,* I mean,—until I have searched to the bottom of it. It is true, there is infinite pleasure in this charitable pursuit. Oh! how delicious to go and condole with the friends of some backsliding sister, or to retire with some old dowager or maiden aunt of the family, who love scandal so well that they cannot forbear gratifying their appetite at the expense of the reputation of their nearest relations! And then to return full fraught with a rich collection of circumstances, to retail to the next circle of our acquaintance under the strongest injunctions of secrecy,—ha, ha, ha!—interlarding the melancholy tale with so many doleful shakes of the head, and more doleful "Ah! who would have thought it! so amiable, so prudent a young lady, as we all thought her, what a monstrous pity! well, I have nothing to charge myself with; I acted the part of a friend, I warned her of the principles of that rake, I told her what would be the consequence; I told her so, I told her so."—Ha, ha, ha!

LETITIA: Ha, ha, ha! Well, but, Charlotte, you don't tell me what you think of Miss Bloomsbury's match.

CHARLOTTE: Think! why I think it is probable she cried for a plaything, and they have given her a husband. Well, well, well, the puling chit shall not be deprived of her plaything: 'tis only exchanging London dolls for American babies.—Apropos, of babies, have you heard what Mrs. Affable's high-flying notions of delicacy have come to?

LETITIA: Who, she that was Miss Lovely?

CHARLOTTE: The same; she married Bob Affable of Schenectady. Don't you remember?

Enter SERVANT.

SERVANT: Madam, the carriage is ready.

LETITIA: Shall we go to the stores first, or visiting?

CHARLOTTE: I should think it rather too early to visit, especially Mrs. Prim; you know she is so particular.

LETITIA: Well, but what of Mrs. Affable?

CHARLOTTE: Oh, I'll tell you as we go; come, come, let us hasten. I hear Mrs. Catgut has some of the prettiest caps arrived you ever saw. I shall die if I have not the first sight of them.

[*Exeunt.*

SCENE II.

A Room in VAN ROUGH's House.
MARIA *sitting disconsolate at a Table, with Books, &c.*

SONG.[8]

I.

The sun sets in night, and the stars shun the day;
But glory remains when their lights fade away!
Begin, ye tormentors! your threats are in vain,
For the son of Alknomook shall never complain.

II.

Remember the arrows he shot from his bow;
Remember your chiefs by his hatchet laid low:
Why so slow?—do you wait till I shrink from the pain?
No—the son of Alknomook will never complain.

---

[8] "Alknomook," an Indian death song describing the heroic endurance and integrity of a dying warrior, was popular in England and America. It was probably written by Anne Home Hunter, an English poet (G. Thomas Tansell, *Royall Tyler* [Cambridge, Mass.: Harvard University Press, 1967], 58–59).

III.

Remember the wood where in ambush we lay,
And the scalps which we bore from your nation away:
Now the flame rises fast, you exult in my pain;
But the son of Alknomook can never complain.

IV.

I go to the land where my father is gone;
His ghost shall rejoice in the fame of his son:
Death comes like a friend, he relieves me from pain;
And thy son, Oh Alknomook! has scorn'd to complain.

There is something in this song which ever calls forth my affections. The manly virtue of courage, that fortitude which steels the heart against the keenest misfortunes, which interweaves the laurel of glory amidst the instruments of torture and death, displays something so noble, so exalted, that in despite of the prejudices of education I cannot but admire it, even in a savage. The prepossession which our sex is supposed to entertain for the character of a soldier is, I know, a standing piece of raillery among the wits. A cockade, a lapell'd coat, and a feather, they will tell you, are irresistible by a female heart. Let it be so. Who is it that considers the helpless situation of our sex, that does not see that we each moment stand in need of a protector, and that a brave one too? Formed of the more delicate materials of nature, endowed only with the softer passions, incapable, from our ignorance of the world, to guard against the wiles of mankind, our security for happiness often depends upon their generosity and courage. Alas! how little of the former do we find! How inconsistent! that man should be leagued to destroy that honour upon which solely rests his respect and esteem. Ten thousand temptations allure us, ten thousand passions betray us; yet the smallest deviation from the path of rectitude is followed by the contempt and insult of man, and the more remorseless pity of woman; years of penitence and tears cannot wash away the stain, nor a life of virtue obliterate its remembrance. Reputation is the life of woman; yet courage to protect it is masculine and disgusting; and the only safe asylum a woman of delicacy can find is in the arms of a man of honour. How naturally, then, should we love the brave and the generous; how gratefully should we bless the arm raised for our protection, when nerv'd by virtue and directed by honour! Heaven grant that the man with whom I may be connected—may be connected! Whither has my imagination transported me—whither does it now lead me? Am I not indissolubly engaged, "by every obligation of honour which my own consent and my father's approbation can give," to a man who can never share my affections, and whom a few days hence it will be criminal for me to disapprove—to disapprove! would to heaven that were all—to despise. For, can the most frivolous manners, actuated by the most depraved heart, meet, or merit, anything but contempt from every woman of delicacy and sentiment?

VAN ROUGH [*without*]: Mary!

Ha! my father's voice—Sir!—

Enter VAN ROUGH.

VAN ROUGH: What, Mary, always singing doleful ditties, and moping over these plaguy books.

MARIA: I hope, Sir, that it is not criminal to improve my mind with books, or to divert my melancholy with singing, at my leisure hours.

VAN ROUGH: Why, I don't know that, child; I don't know that. They us'd to say, when I was a young man, that if a woman knew how to make a pudding, and to keep herself out of fire and water, she knew enough for a wife. Now, what good have these books done you? have they not made you melancholy? as you call it. Pray, what right has a girl of your age to be in the dumps? haven't you everything your heart can wish; an't you going to be married to a young man of great fortune; an't you going to have the quit-rent[9] of twenty miles square?

MARIA: One-hundredth part of the land, and a lease for life of the heart of a man I could love, would satisfy me.

VAN ROUGH: Pho, pho, pho! child; nonsense, downright nonsense, child. This comes of your reading your story-books; your Charles Gran-

---

[9] Quitrent: a fee (or rent) freemen paid for the use of land in lieu of services required by feudal custom. Colonial New York had several large tenanted estates, known as "manors," which remained intact after the Revolution.

disons, your Sentimental Journals, and your Robinson Crusoes, and such other trumpery. No, no, no! child; it is money makes the mare go; keep your eye upon the main chance, Mary.

MARIA: Marriage, Sir, is, indeed, a very serious affair.

VAN ROUGH: You are right, child; you are right. I am sure I found it so, to my cost.

MARIA: I mean, Sir, that as marriage is a portion for life, and so intimately involves our happiness, we cannot be too considerate in the choice of our companion.

VAN ROUGH: Right, child; very right. A young woman should be very sober when she is making her choice, but when she has once made it, as you have done, I don't see why she should not be as merry as a grig; I am sure she has reason enough to be so. Solomon says that "there is a time to laugh, and a time to weep."[10] Now, a time for a young woman to laugh is when she has made sure of a good rich husband. Now, a time to cry, according to you, Mary, is when she is making choice of him; but I should think that a young woman's time to cry was when she despaired of *getting* one. Why, there was your mother, now: to be sure, when I popp'd the question to her she did look a little silly; but when she had once looked down on her apron-strings, as all modest young women us'd to do, and drawled out ye-s, she was as brisk and as merry as a bee.

MARIA: My honoured mother, Sir, had no motive to melancholy; she married the man of her choice.

VAN ROUGH: The man of her choice! And pray, Mary, an't you going to marry the man of your choice—what trumpery notion is this? It is these vile books [*throwing them away*]. I'd have you to know, Mary, if you won't make young Van Dumpling the man of *your* choice, you shall marry him as the man of *my* choice.

MARIA: You terrify me, Sir. Indeed, Sir, I am all submission. My will is yours.

VAN ROUGH: Why, that is the way your mother us'd to talk. "My will is yours, my dear Mr. Van Rough, my will is yours"; but she took special care to have her own way, though, for all that.

MARIA: Do not reflect upon my mother's memory, Sir—

VAN ROUGH: Why not, Mary, why not? She kept me from speaking my

[10] Ecclesiastes 3:4.

mind all her *life,* and do you think she shall henpeck me now she is *dead* too? Come, come; don't go to sniveling; be a good girl, and mind the main chance. I'll see you well settled in the world.

MARIA: I do not doubt your love, Sir, and it is my duty to obey you. I will endeavour to make my duty and inclination go hand in hand.

VAN ROUGH: Well, well, Mary; do you be a good girl, mind the main chance, and never mind inclination. Why, do you know that I have been down in the cellar this very morning to examine a pipe of Madeira[11] which I purchased the week you were born, and mean to tap on your wedding day?—That pipe cost me fifty pounds sterling. It was well worth sixty pounds; but I over-reach'd Ben Bulkhead, the supercargo.[12] I'll tell you the whole story. You must know that—

Enter SERVANT.

SERVANT: Sir, Mr. Transfer, the broker is below.

[*Exit.*

VAN ROUGH: Well, Mary, I must go. Remember, and be a good girl, and mind the main chance.

[*Exit.*

MARIA *alone:* How deplorable is my situation! How distressing for a daughter to find her heart militating with her filial duty! I know my father loves me tenderly; why then do I reluctantly obey him? Heaven knows! with what reluctance I should oppose the will of a parent, or set an example of filial disobedience; at a parent's command, I could wed awkwardness and deformity. Were the heart of my husband good, I would so magnify his good qualities with the eye of conjugal affection, that the defects of his person and manners should be lost in the emanation of his virtues. At a father's command, I could embrace poverty. Were the poor man my husband, I

---

[11] Madeira: fortified wine imported from the island of Madeira. A pipe was a cask used to transport and store wine and had a capacity of approximately 126 gallons.

[12] Supercargo: an officer on a merchant ship who was responsible for its cargo and related financial transactions.

would learn resignation to my lot; I would enliven our frugal meal with good humour, and chase away misfortune from our cottage with a smile. At a father's command, I could almost submit to what every female heart knows to be the most mortifying, to marry a weak man, and blush at my husband's folly in every company I visited. But to marry a depraved wretch, whose only virtue is a polished exterior; who is actuated by the unmanly ambition of conquering the defence-less; whose heart, insensible to the emotions of patriotism, dilates at the plaudits of every unthinking girl; whose laurels are the sighs and tears of the miserable victims of his specious behaviour,—can he, who has no regard for the peace and happiness of other families, ever have a due regard for the peace and happiness of his own? Would to heaven that my father were not so hasty in his temper? Surely, if I were to state my reasons for declining this match, he would not compel me to marry a man, whom, though my lips may solemnly promise to honour, I find my heart must ever despise.

[*Exit.*

End of the First Act.

Act II.

SCENE I.

Enter CHARLOTTE and LETITIA.

CHARLOTTE [*at entering*]: Betty, take those things out of the carriage and carry them to my chamber; see that you don't tumble them. My dear, I protest, I think it was the homeliest of the whole. I declare I was almost tempted to return and change it.

LETITIA: Why would you take it?

CHARLOTTE: Didn't Mrs. Catgut say it was the most fashionable?

LETITIA: But, my dear, it will never fit becomingly on you.

CHARLOTTE: I know that; but did you not hear Mrs. Catgut say it was fashionable?

LETITIA: Did you see that sweet airy cap with the white sprig?

CHARLOTTE: Yes, and I longed to take it; but, my dear, what could I do? Did not Mrs. Catgut say it was the most fashionable; and if I had not taken it, was not that awkward gawky, Sally Slender, ready to purchase it immediately?

LETITIA: Did you observe how she tumbled over the things at the next shop, and then went off without purchasing anything, nor even thanking the poor man for his trouble? But, of all the awkward creatures, did you see Miss Blouze endeavouring to thrust her unmerciful arm into those small kid gloves?

CHARLOTTE: Ha, ha, ha, ha!

LETITIA: Then did you take notice with what an affected warmth of friendship she and Miss Wasp met? when all their acquaintance know how much pleasure they take in abusing each other in every company.

CHARLOTTE: Lud![13] Letitia, is that so extraordinary? Why, my dear, I hope you are not going to turn sentimentalist. Scandal, you know, is but amusing ourselves with the faults, foibles, follies, and reputations of our friends; indeed, I don't know why we should have friends, if we are not at liberty to make use of them. But no person is so ignorant of the world as to suppose, because I amuse myself with a lady's

---

[13] Lud: Lord.

faults, that I am obliged to quarrel with her person every time we meet: believe me, my dear, we should have very few acquaintance at that rate.

SERVANT *enters and delivers a letter to* CHARLOTTE, *and—[Exit.*

CHARLOTTE: You'll excuse me, my dear. [*Opens and reads to herself.*
LETITIA: Oh, quite excusable.
CHARLOTTE: As I hope to be married, my brother Henry is in the city.
LETITIA: What, your brother, Colonel Manly?
CHARLOTTE: Yes, my dear; the only brother I have in the world.
LETITIA: Was he never in this city?
CHARLOTTE: Never nearer than Harlem Heights,[14] where he lay with his regiment.
LETITIA: What sort of a being is this brother of yours? If he is as chatty, as pretty, as sprightly as you, half the belles in the city will be pulling caps[15] for him.
CHARLOTTE: My brother is the very counterpart and reverse of me: I am gay, he is grave; I am airy, he is solid; I am ever selecting the most pleasing objects for my laughter, he has a tear for every pitiful one. And thus, whilst he is plucking the briars and thorns from the path of the unfortunate, I am strewing my own path with roses.
LETITIA: My sweet friend, not quite so poetical, and a little more particular.
CHARLOTTE: Hands off, Letitia. I feel the rage of simile upon me; I can't talk to you in any other way. My brother has a heart replete with the noblest sentiments, but then, it is like—it is like—Oh! you provoking girl, you have deranged all my ideas—it is like—Oh! I have it—his heart is like an old maiden lady's band-box;[16] it contains many costly things, arranged with the most scrupulous nicety, yet the misfortune is that they are too delicate, costly, and antiquated for common use.
LETITIA: By what I can pick out of your flowery description, your brother is no beau.

---

[14] Harlem Heights, at the northern end of Manhattan Island, was the site of a minor battle, won by American forces, on 16 September 1776.
[15] Pulling caps: undignified quarrelling that involved pulling off each other's hats or caps.
[16] Band-box: a box for storing collars, bands, caps, ribbons, and other ornaments.

CHARLOTTE: No, indeed; he makes no pretension to the character. He'd ride, or rather fly, an hundred miles to relieve a distressed object, or to do a gallant act in the service of his country; but should you drop your fan or bouquet in his presence, it is ten to one that some beau at the farther end of the room would have the honour of presenting it to you before he had observed that it fell. I'll tell you one of his anti-quated, anti-gallant notions. He said once in my presence, in a room full of company,—would you believe it?—in a large circle of ladies, that the best evidence a gentleman could give a young lady of his re-spect and affection was to endeavour in a friendly manner to rectify her foibles. I protest I was crimson to the eyes, upon reflecting that I was known as his sister.

LETITIA: Insupportable creature! tell a lady of her faults! if he is so grave, I fear I have no chance of captivating him.

CHARLOTTE: His conversation is like a rich, old-fashioned brocade,—it will stand alone; every sentence is a sentiment. Now you may judge what a time I had with him, in my twelve months' visit to my father. He read me such lectures, out of pure brotherly affection, against the extremes of fashion, dress, flirting, and coquetry, and all the other dear things which he knows I doat upon, that I protest his conversa-tion made me as melancholy as if I had been at church; and heaven knows, though I never prayed to go there but on one occasion, yet I would have exchanged his conversation for a psalm and a sermon. Church is rather melancholy, to be sure; but then I can ogle the beaux, and be regaled with "here endeth the first lesson," but his brotherly *here,* you would think had no end. You captivate him! Why, my dear, he would as soon fall in love with a box of Italian flowers. There is Maria, now, if she were not engaged, she might do something. Oh! how I should like to see that pair of pensorosos[17] to-gether, looking as grave as two sailors' wives of a stormy night, with a flow of sentiment meandering through their conversation like purl-ing streams in modern poetry.

LETITIA: Oh! my dear fanciful—

CHARLOTTE: Hush! I hear some person coming through the entry.

Enter SERVANT.

[17] Pensorosos [penserosos]: brooding or melancholy persons.

SERVANT: Madam, there's a gentleman below who calls himself Colonel Manly; do you chuse to be at home?

CHARLOTTE: Shew him in. [*Exit* SERVANT.] Now for a sober face.

Enter Colonel MANLY.

MANLY: My dear Charlotte, I am happy that I once more enfold you within the arms of fraternal affection. I know you are going to ask (amiable impatience!) how our parents do,—the venerable pair transmit you their blessing by me. They totter on the verge of a well-spent life, and wish only to see their children settled in the world, to depart in peace.

CHARLOTTE: I am very happy to hear that they are well. [*Coolly.*] Brother, will you give me leave to introduce you to our uncle's ward, one of my most intimate friends?

MANLY [*saluting* LETITIA]: I ought to regard your friends as my own.

CHARLOTTE: Come, Letitia, do give us a little dash of your vivacity; my brother is so sentimental and so grave, that I protest he'll give us the vapours.

MANLY: Though sentiment and gravity, I know, are banished the polite world, yet I hoped they might find some countenance in the meeting of such near connections as brother and sister.

CHARLOTTE: Positively, brother, if you go one step further in this strain, you will set me crying, and that, you know, would spoil my eyes; and then I should never get the husband which our good papa and mamma have so kindly wished me—never be established in the world.

MANLY: Forgive me, my sister,—I am no enemy to mirth; I love your sprightliness; and I hope it will one day enliven the hours of some worthy man; but when I mention the respectable authors of my existence,—the cherishers and protectors of my helpless infancy, whose hearts glow with such fondness and attachment that they would willingly lay down their lives for my welfare,—you will excuse me if I am so unfashionable as to speak of them with some degree of respect and reverence.

CHARLOTTE: Well, well, brother; if you won't be gay, we'll not differ; I will be as grave as you wish. [*Affects gravity.*] And so, brother, you have come to the city to exchange some of your commutation notes for a little pleasure?

MANLY: Indeed you are mistaken; my errand is not of amusement, but business; and as I neither drink nor game, my expenses will be so trivial, I shall have no occasion to sell my notes.[18]

CHARLOTTE: Then you won't have occasion to do a very good thing. Why, here was the Vermont General[19]—he came down some time since, sold all his musty notes at one stroke, and then laid the cash out in trinkets for his dear Fanny. I want a dozen pretty things myself; have you got the notes with you?

MANLY: I shall be ever willing to contribute, as far as it is in my power, to adorn or in any way to please my sister; yet I hope I shall never be obliged for this to sell my notes. I may be romantic, but I preserve them as a sacred deposit. Their full amount is justly due to me, but as embarrassments, the natural consequences of a long war, disable my country from supporting its credit, I shall wait with patience until it is rich enough to discharge them. If that is not in my day, they shall be transmitted as an honourable certificate to posterity, that I have humbly imitated our illustrious WASHINGTON, in having exposed my health and life in the service of my country, without reaping any other reward than the glory of conquering in so arduous a contest.

CHARLOTTE: Well said heroics. Why, my dear Henry, you have such a lofty way of saying things, that I protest I almost tremble at the thought of introducing you to the polite circles in the city. The belles would think you were a player run mad, with your head filled with old scraps of tragedy; and as to the beaux, they might admire, because they would not understand you. But, however, I must, I believe, introduce you to two or three ladies of my acquaintance.

LETITIA: And that will make him acquainted with thirty or forty beaux.

CHARLOTTE: Oh! brother, you don't know what a fund of happiness you have in store.

---

[18] Charlotte and Manly refer to promissory notes that soldiers and public creditors received from revolutionary era governments in lieu of payment for goods and services. Their value plummeted, as public debts remained unpaid in the 1780s. Manly's resolve to keep his notes signifies his patriotism and optimism for the future of the republic.

[19] Ethan Allen was a revolutionary hero and populist leader of Vermont's ultimately successful effort to separate from New York and become the fourteenth state. Allen married Frances Buchanan of New York City in 1783. Most elite New Yorkers would have regarded Allen, who sympathized with the insurgents in western Massachusetts, as a dangerous demagogue. See Michael A. Bellesiles, *Revolutionary Outlaws: Ethan Allen and the Struggle for Independence on the Vermont Frontier* (Charlottesville: University Press of Virginia, 1993), esp. 252–54.

MANLY: I fear, sister, I have not refinement sufficient to enjoy it.

CHARLOTTE: Oh! you cannot fail being pleased.

LETITIA: Our ladies are so delicate and dressy.

CHARLOTTE: And our beaux so dressy and delicate.

LETITIA: Our ladies chat and flirt so agreeably.

CHARLOTTE: And our beaux simper and bow so gracefully.

LETITIA: With their hair so trim and neat.

CHARLOTTE: And their faces so soft and sleek.

LETITIA: Their buckles so tonish and bright.

CHARLOTTE: And their hands so slender and white.

LETITIA: I vow, Charlotte, we are quite poetical.

CHARLOTTE: And then, brother, the faces of the beaux are of such a lily-white hue! None of that horrid robustness of constitution, that vulgar corn-fed glow of health, which can only serve to alarm an unmarried lady with apprehension, and prove a melancholy memento to a married one, that she can never hope for the happiness of being a widow. I will say this to the credit of our city beaux, that such is the delicacy of their complexion, dress, and address, that, even had I no reliance upon the honour of the dear Adonises, I would trust myself in any possible situation with them, without the least apprehensions of rudeness.

MANLY: Sister Charlotte!

CHARLOTTE: Now, now, now, brother [*interrupting him*], now don't go to spoil my mirth with a dash of your gravity; I am so glad to see you, I am in tiptop spirits. Oh! that you could be with us at a little snug party. There is Billy Simper, Jack Chaffé, and Colonel Van Titter, Miss Promonade, and the two Miss Tambours, sometimes make a party, with some other ladies, in a side-box at the play. Everything is conducted with such decorum. First we bow round to the company in general, then to each one in particular, then we have so many inquiries after each other's health, and we are so happy to meet each other, and it is so many ages since we last had that pleasure, and if a married lady is in company, we have such a sweet dissertation upon her son Bobby's chin-cough; then the curtain rises, then our sensibility is all awake, and then, by the mere force of apprehension, we torture some harmless expression into a double meaning, which the poor author never dreamt of, and then we have recourse to our fans, and then we blush, and then the gentlemen jog one another, peep under the fan, and make the prettiest remarks; and then we giggle and they simper, and they giggle and we simper, and then the curtain drops, and then for nuts and oranges, and then we bow, and it's pray, Ma'am, take it, and pray, Sir, keep it, and oh! not for the world, Sir; and then the curtain rises again, and then we blush and giggle and simper and bow all over again. Oh! the sentimental charms of a side-box conversation!

[*All laugh.*]

MANLY: Well, sister, I join heartily with you in the laugh; for, in my opinion, it is as justifiable to laugh at folly as it is reprehensible to ridicule misfortune.

CHARLOTTE: Well, but, brother, positively I can't introduce you in these clothes: why, your coat looks as if it were calculated for the vulgar purpose of keeping yourself comfortable.

MANLY: This coat was my regimental coat in the late war. The public tumults of our state[20] have induced me to buckle on the sword in support of that government which I once fought to establish. I can only say, sister, that there was a time when this coat was respectable, and some people even thought that those men who had endured so many winter campaigns in the service of their country, without bread, clothing, or pay, at least deserved that the poverty of their appearance should not be ridiculed.

CHARLOTTE: We agree in opinion entirely, brother, though it would not have done for me to have said it: it is the coat makes the man respectable. In the time of the war, when we were almost frightened to death, why, your coat was respectable, that is, fashionable; now another kind of coat is fashionable, that is, respectable. And pray direct the taylor to make yours the height of the fashion.

MANLY: Though it is of little consequence to me of what shape my coat is, yet, as to the height of the fashion, there you will please to excuse me, sister. You know my sentiments on that subject. I have often lamented the advantage which the French have over us in that particular. In Paris, the fashions have their dawnings, their routine, and declensions, and depend as much upon the caprice of the day as in other countries; but there every lady assumes a right to deviate from

---

[20] Shays's Rebellion.

the general *ton* as far as will be of advantage to her own appearance. In America, the cry is, what is the fashion? and we follow it indiscriminately, because it is so.

CHARLOTTE: Therefore it is, that when large hoops are in fashion, we often see many a plump girl lost in the immensity of a hoop-petticoat, whose want of height and *en-bon-point* would never have been remarked in any other dress. When the high head-dress is the mode, how then do we see a lofty cushion, with a profusion of gauze, feathers, and ribband, supported by a face no bigger than an apple! whilst a broad full-faced lady, who really would have appeared tolerably handsome in a large head-dress, looks with her smart chapeau as masculine as a soldier.

MANLY: But remember, my dear sister, and I wish all my fair countrywomen would recollect, that the only excuse a young lady can have for going extravagantly into a fashion is because it makes her look extravagantly handsome.—Ladies, I must wish you a good morning.

CHARLOTTE: But, brother, you are going to make home with us.

MANLY: Indeed I cannot. I have seen my uncle and explained that matter.

CHARLOTTE: Come and dine with us, then. We have a family dinner about half-past four o'clock.

MANLY: I am engaged to dine with the Spanish ambassador. I was introduced to him by an old brother officer; and instead of freezing me with a cold card of compliment to dine with him ten days hence, he, with the true old Castilian frankness, in a friendly manner, asked me to dine with him to-day—an honour I could not refuse. Sister, adieu —Madam, your most obedient—

[*Exit.*

CHARLOTTE: I will wait upon you to the door, brother; I have something particular to say to you.

[*Exit.*

LETITIA *alone:* What a pair!—She the pink of flirtation, he the essence of everything that is *outré* and gloomy.—I think I have completely deceived Charlotte by my manner of speaking of Mr. Dimple; she's too much the friend of Maria to be confided in. He is certainly rendering

himself disagreeable to Maria, in order to break with her and proffer his hand to me. This is what the delicate fellow hinted in our last
conversation.

[*Exit.*

SCENE II.

The Mall.

Enter JESSAMY: Positively this Mall is a very pretty place. I hope the cits
won't ruin it by repairs. To be sure, it won't do to speak of in the
same day with Ranelagh or Vauxhall;[21] however, it's a fine place for a
young fellow to display his person to advantage. Indeed, nothing is
lost here; the girls have taste, and I am very happy to find they have
adopted the elegant London fashion of looking back, after a genteel
fellow like me has passed them.—Ah! who comes here? This, by his
awkwardness, must be the Yankee colonel's servant. I'll accost him.

Enter JONATHAN.

JESSAMY: Votre très-humble serviteur, Monsieur. I understand Colonel
Manly, the Yankee officer, has the honour of your services.
JONATHAN: Sir!—
JESSAMY: I say, Sir, I understand that Colonel Manly has the honour of
having you for a servant.
JONATHAN: Servant! Sir, do you take me for a neger,—I am Colonel
Manly's waiter.
JESSAMY: A true Yankee distinction, egad, without a difference. Why,
Sir, do you not perform all the offices of a servant? do you not even
blacken his boots?
JONATHAN: Yes; I do grease them a bit sometimes; but I am a true blue
son of liberty, for all that. Father said I should come as Colonel
Manly's waiter, to see the world, and all that; but no man shall mas-
ter me. My father has as good a farm as the colonel.
JESSAMY: Well, Sir, we will not quarrel about terms upon the eve of an

---

[21] Ranelagh and Vauxhall were fashionable pleasure gardens in London. "Cits" was a
contemptuous term for "citizens," who may have resented New York's Mall, or promenade, as the site of ostentatious display by local elites.

acquaintance from which I promise myself so much satisfaction;—
therefore, sans ceremonie—

JONATHAN: What?—

JESSAMY: I say I am extremely happy to see Colonel Manly's waiter.

JONATHAN: Well, and I vow, too, I am pretty considerably glad to see
you; but what the dogs need of all this outlandish lingo? Who may
you be, Sir, if I may be so bold?

JESSAMY: I have the honour to be Mr. Dimple's servant, or, if you please,
waiter. We lodge under the same roof, and should be glad of the honour of your acquaintance.

JONATHAN: You a waiter! by the living jingo, you look so topping, I
took you for one of the agents to Congress.

JESSAMY: The brute has discernment, notwithstanding his appearance.
—Give me leave to say I wonder then at your familiarity.

JONATHAN: Why, as to the matter of that, Mr.—; pray, what's your
name?

JESSAMY: Jessamy, at your service.

JONATHAN: Why, I swear we don't make any great matter of distinction
in our state between quality and other folks.

JESSAMY: This is, indeed, a levelling principle.—I hope, Mr. Jonathan,
you have not taken part with the insurgents.

JONATHAN: Why, since General Shays has sneaked off and given us the
bag to hold, I don't care to give my opinion; but you'll promise not
to tell—put your ear this way—you won't tell?—I vow I did think
the sturgeons[22] were right.

JESSAMY: I thought, Mr. Jonathan, you Massachusetts men always argued with a gun in your hand. Why didn't you join them?

JONATHAN: Why, the colonel is one of those folks called the Shin—Shin
—dang it all,[23] I can't speak them lignum vitae words—you know
who I mean—there is a company of them—they wear a china goose
at their button-hole—a kind of gilt thing.—Now the colonel told
father and brother,—you must know there are, let me see—there is

[22] The term "sturgeons" (insurgents) refers to participants in Shays's Rebellion.

[23] The Society of the Cincinnati, or "Shin-Shin," founded in 1783, was open to all
men who had been officers in the Continental Army and their descendants. The group's
exclusiveness and hereditary membership led critics to condemn it as aristocratic and antithetic to republicanism (Charles Royster, *A Revolutionary People at War: The Continental
Army and the American Character, 1775–1783* [Chapel Hill: University of North Carolina Press, 1979], 353–57).

Elnathan, Silas, and Barnabas, Tabitha—no, no, she's a she—tarnation, now I have it—there's Elnathan, Silas, Barnabas, Jonathan,
that's I—seven of us, six went into the wars, and I staid at home to
take care of mother. Colonel said that it was a burning shame for
the true blue Bunker Hill sons of liberty, who had fought Governor
Hutchinson, Lord North, and the Devil, to have any hand in kicking
up a cursed dust against a government which we had, every mother's
son of us, a hand in making.

JESSAMY: Bravo!—Well, have you been abroad in the city since your ar-
rival? What have you seen that is curious and entertaining?

JONATHAN: Oh! I have seen a power of fine sights. I went to see two
marble-stone men and a leaden horse that stands out in doors in all
weathers; and when I came where they was, one had got no head,
and t'other wern't there. They said as how the leaden man was a
damn'd tory,[24] and that he took wit in his anger and rode off in the
time of the troubles.

JESSAMY: But this was not the end of your excursion?

JONATHAN: Oh, no; I went to a place they call Holy Ground.[25] Now I
counted this was a place where folks go to meeting; so I put my
hymn-book in my pocket, and walked softly and grave as a minister;
and when I came there, the dogs a bit of a meeting-house could I see.
At last I spied a young gentlewoman standing by one of the seats
which they have here at the doors. I took her to be the deacon's
daughter, and she looked so kind, and so obliging, that I thought I
would go and ask her the way to lecture, and—would you think it?
—she called me dear, and sweeting, and honey, just as if we were
married: by the living jingo, I had a month's mind to buss[26] her.

JESSAMY: Well, but how did it end?

JONATHAN: Why, as I was standing talking with her, a parcel of sailor
men and boys got round me, the snarl-headed curs fell a-kicking and
cursing of me at such a tarnal rate, that I vow I was glad to take to
my heels and split home, right off, tail on end, like a stream of chalk.

---

[24] Tory: an American colonist who remained loyal to King George III after the Declaration of Independence.

[25] Church Farm, near St. Paul's Chapel in lower Manhattan, was the site of Holy
Ground, center of the sex trade in eighteenth-century New York and home to as many as
500 prostitutes (Edwin G. Burrows and Mike Wallace, *Gotham: A History of New York
City to 1898* [New York: Oxford University Press, 1999], 214).

[26] Buss: kiss.

JESSAMY: Why, my dear friend, you are not acquainted with the city; that girl you saw was a—[*whispers.*]

JONATHAN: Mercy on my soul! was that young woman a harlot!—Well! if this is New-York Holy Ground, what must the Holy-day Ground be!

JESSAMY: Well, you should not judge of the city too rashly. We have a number of elegant, fine girls here that make a man's leisure hours pass very agreeably. I would esteem it an honour to announce you to some of them.—Gad! that announce is a select word; I wonder where I picked it up.

JONATHAN: I don't want to know them.

JESSAMY: Come, come, my dear friend, I see that I must assume the honour of being the director of your amusements. Nature has given us passions, and youth and opportunity stimulate to gratify them. It is no shame, my dear Blueskin,[27] for a man to amuse himself with a little gallantry.

JONATHAN: Girl huntry! I don't altogether understand. I never played at that game. I know how to play hunt the squirrel, but I can't play anything with the girls; I am as good as married.

JESSAMY: Vulgar, horrid brute! Married, and above a hundred miles from his wife, and thinks that an objection to his making love to every woman he meets! He never can have read, no, he never can have been in a room with a volume of the divine Chesterfield.—So you are married?

JONATHAN: No, I don't say so; I said I was as good as married, a kind of promise.

JESSAMY: As good as married!—

JONATHAN: Why, yes; there's Tabitha Wymen, the deacon's daughter, at home; she and I have been courting a great while, and folks say as how we are to be married; and so I broke a piece of money with her when we parted, and she promised not to spark it with Solomon Dyer while I am gone. You wouldn't have me false to my true-love, would you?

JESSAMY: May be you have another reason for constancy; possibly the young lady has a fortune? Ha! Mr. Jonathan, the solid charms: the chains of love are never so binding as when the links are made of gold.

---

[27] Blueskin: a nickname for Calvinists, especially Presbyterians, due to their supposed coldness and gravity.

JONATHAN: Why, as to fortune, I must needs say her father is pretty dumb rich; he went representative for our town last year. He will give her—let me see—four times seven is—seven times four—nought and carry one,—he will give her twenty acres of land—somewhat rocky though—a Bible, and a cow.

JESSAMY: Twenty acres of rock, a Bible, and a cow! Why, my dear Mr. Jonathan, we have servant-maids, or, as you would more elegantly express it, waitresses, in this city, who collect more in one year from their mistresses' cast clothes.

JONATHAN: You don't say so!—

JESSAMY: Yes, and I'll introduce you to one of them. There is a little lump of flesh and delicacy that lives at next door, waitress to Miss Maria; we often see her on the stoop.

JONATHAN: But are you sure she would be courted by me?

JESSAMY: Never doubt it; remember a faint heart never—blisters on my tongue—I was going to be guilty of a vile proverb; flat against the authority of Chesterfield. I say there can be no doubt that the brilliancy of your merit will secure you a favourable reception.

JONATHAN: Well, but what must I say to her?

JESSAMY: Say to her! why, my dear friend, though I admire your profound knowledge on every other subject, yet, you will pardon my saying that your want of opportunity has made the female heart escape the poignancy of your penetration. Say to her! Why, when a man goes a-courting, and hopes for success, he must begin with doing, and not saying.

JONATHAN: Well, what must I do?

JESSAMY: Why, when you are introduced you must make five or six elegant bows.

JONATHAN: Six elegant bows! I understand that; six, you say? Well—

JESSAMY: Then you must press and kiss her hand; then press and kiss, and so on to her lips and cheeks; then talk as much as you can about hearts, darts, flames, nectar, and ambrosia—the more incoherent the better.

JONATHAN: Well, but suppose she should be angry with I?

JESSAMY: Why, if she should pretend—please to observe, Mr. Jonathan —if she should pretend to be offended, you must—But I'll tell you how my master acted in such a case: He was seated by a young lady of eighteen upon a sofa, plucking with a wanton hand the blooming sweets of youth and beauty. When the lady thought it necessary to

check his ardour, she called up a frown upon her lovely face, so irre-
sistibly alluring, that it would have warmed the frozen bosom of age;
remember, said she, putting her delicate arm upon his, remember
your character and my honour. My master instantly dropped upon
his knees, with eyes swimming with love, cheeks glowing with desire,
and in the gentlest modulation of voice he said: My dear Caroline, in
a few months our hands will be indissolubly united at the altar; our
hearts I feel are already so; the favours you now grant as evidence of
your affection are favours indeed; yet, when the ceremony is once
past, what will now be received with rapture will then be attributed
to duty.

JONATHAN: Well, and what was the consequence?

JESSAMY: The consequence!—Ah! forgive me, my dear friend, but you
New England gentlemen have such a laudable curiosity of seeing the
bottom of everything;—why, to be honest, I confess I saw the blooming cherub of a consequence smiling in its angelic mother's arms,
about ten months afterwards.

JONATHAN: Well, if I follow all your plans, make them six bows, and all
that, shall I have such little cherubim consequences?

JESSAMY: Undoubtedly.—What are you musing upon?

JONATHAN: You say you'll certainly make me acquainted?—Why, I was
thinking then how I should contrive to pass this broken piece of sil-
ver—won't it buy a sugar-dram?

JESSAMY: What is that, the love-token from the deacon's daughter?—You
come on bravely. But I must hasten to my master. Adieu, my dear
friend.

JONATHAN: Stay, Mr. Jessamy—must I buss her when I am introduced
to her?

JESSAMY: I told you, you must kiss her.

JONATHAN: Well, but must I buss her?

JESSAMY: Why, kiss and buss, and buss and kiss, is all one.

JONATHAN: Oh! my dear friend, though you have a profound knowledge of all, a pugency of tribulation, you don't know everything.

[*Exit.*

JESSAMY *alone:* Well, certainly I improve; my master could not have insinuated himself with more address into the heart of a man he de-
spised. Now will this blundering dog sicken Jenny with his nauseous

pawings, until she flies into my arms for very ease. How sweet will the contrast be between the blundering Jonathan and the courtly and accomplished Jessamy!

End of the Second Act.

Act III.

SCENE I.

DIMPLE's *Room.*

DIMPLE *discovered at a Toilet, Reading*: "Women have in general but one object, which is their beauty." Very true, my lord; positively very true. "Nature has hardly formed a woman ugly enough to be insensible to flattery upon her person." Extremely just, my lord; every day's delightful experience confirms this. "If her face is so shocking that she must, in some degree, be conscious of it, her figure and air, she thinks, make ample amends for it." The sallow Miss Wan is a proof of this. Upon my telling the distasteful wretch, the other day, that her countenance spoke the pensive language of sentiment, and that Lady Wortley Montague declared that if the ladies were arrayed in the garb of innocence, the face would be the last part which would be admired, as Monsieur Milton expresses it; she grinn'd horribly, a ghastly smile. "If her figure is deformed, she thinks her face counterbalances it."[28]

Enter JESSAMY *with letters.*

DIMPLE: Where got you these, Jessamy?
JESSAMY: Sir, the English packet[29] is arrived.

DIMPLE *opens and reads a letter enclosing notes*:

"Sir, I have drawn bills on you in favour of Messrs. Van Cash and Co. as per margin. I have taken up your note to Col. Piquet, and discharged your debts to my Lord Lurcher and Sir Harry Rook. I herewith enclose you copies of the bills, which I have no doubt will be immediately honoured. On failure, I shall empower some lawyer in your country to recover the amounts.
  I am, Sir,
  Your most humble servant,
  John Hazard."

---

[28] Dimple reads one of Chesterfield's most notorious passages. John Milton (1608–1674) and Lady Mary Wortley Montague (1689–1762) were English poets.

[29] English packet: packet-boat, or a ship that carries mail.

Now, did not my lord expressly say that it was unbecoming a well-bred man to be in a passion, I confess I should be ruffled. [*Reads.*] "There is no accident so unfortunate, which a wise man may not turn to his advantage; nor any accident so fortunate, which a fool will not turn to his disadvantage." True, my lord; but how advantage can be derived from this I can't see. Chesterfield himself, who made, however, the worst practice of the most excellent precepts, was never in so embarrassing a situation. I love the person of Charlotte, and it is necessary I should command the fortune of Letitia. As to Maria! —I doubt not by my *sang-froid*[30] behaviour I shall compel her to decline the match; but the blame must not fall upon me. A prudent man, as my lord says, should take all the credit of a good action to himself, and throw the discredit of a bad one upon others. I must break with Maria, marry Letitia, and as for Charlotte—why, Charlotte must be a companion to my wife.—Here, Jessamy!

Enter JESSAMY.
DIMPLE *folds and seals two letters.*

DIMPLE: Here, Jessamy, take this letter to my love. [*Gives one.*

JESSAMY: To which of your honour's loves?—Oh! [*reading*] to Miss Letitia, your honour's rich love.

DIMPLE: And this [*delivers another*] to Miss Charlotte Manly. See that you deliver them privately.

JESSAMY: Yes, your honour. [*Going.*

DIMPLE: Jessamy, who are these strange lodgers that came to the house last night?

JESSAMY: Why, the master is a Yankee colonel; I have not seen much of him; but the man is the most unpolished animal your honour ever disgraced your eyes by looking upon. I have had one of the most *outré* conversations with him!—He really has a most prodigious effect upon my risibility.[31]

DIMPLE: I ought, according to every rule of Chesterfield, to wait on him and insinuate myself into his good graces.—Jessamy, wait on the colonel with my compliments, and if he is disengaged I will do myself

---

[30] *Sang-froid:* calm or nonchalant.
[31] Risibility: disposition to laugh.

the honour of paying him my respects.—Some ignorant, unpolished boor—

JESSAMY *goes off and returns.*

JESSAMY: Sir, the colonel is gone out, and Jonathan his servant says that he is gone to stretch his legs upon the Mall.—Stretch his legs! what an indelicacy of diction!

DIMPLE: Very well. Reach me my hat and sword. I'll accost him there, in my way to Letitia's, as by accident; pretend to be struck by his person and address, and endeavour to steal into his confidence. Jessamy, I have no business for you at present.

[*Exit.*

JESSAMY [*taking up the book*]: My master and I obtain our knowledge from the same source;—though, gad! I think myself much the prettier fellow of the two. [*Surveying himself in the glass.*] That was a brilliant thought, to insinuate that I folded my master's letters for him; the folding is so neat, that it does honour to the operator. I once intended to have insinuated that I wrote his letters too; but that was before I saw them; it won't do now; no honour there, positively.— [*Reading affectedly*] "Nothing looks more vulgar, ordinary, and illiberal than ugly, uneven, and ragged nails; the ends of which should be kept even and clean, not tipped with black, and cut in small segments of circles."—Segments of circles! surely my lord did not consider that he wrote for the beaux. Segments of circles; what a crabbed term! Now I dare answer that my master, with all his learning, does not know that this means, according to the present mode, let the nails grow long, and then cut them off even at top. [*Laughing without.*] Ha! that's Jenny's titter. I protest I despair of ever teaching that girl to laugh; she has something so execrably natural in her laugh, that I declare it absolutely discomposes my nerves. How came she into our house! [*Calls.*] Jenny!

Enter JENNY.

JESSAMY: Prythee, Jenny, don't spoil your fine face with laughing.

JENNY: Why, mustn't I laugh, Mr. Jessamy?

JESSAMY: You may smile, but, as my lord says, nothing can authorise a laugh.

JENNY: Well, but I can't help laughing.—Have you seen him, Mr. Jessamy? ha, ha, ha!

JESSAMY: Seen whom?

JENNY: Why, Jonathan, the New England colonel's servant. Do you know he was at the play last night, and the stupid creature don't know where he has been. He would not go to a play for the world; he thinks it was a show, as he calls it.

JESSAMY: As ignorant and unpolished as he is, do you know, Miss Jenny, that I propose to introduce him to the honour of your acquaintance?

JENNY: Introduce him to me! for what?

JESSAMY: Why, my lovely girl, that you may take him under your protection, as Madame Rambouilliet did young Stanhope;[32] that you may, by your plastic hand, mould this uncouth cub into a gentleman. He is to make love to you.

JENNY: Make love to me!—

JESSAMY: Yes, Mistress Jenny, make love to you; and, I doubt not, when he shall become domesticated in your kitchen, that this boor, under your auspices, will soon become un amiable petit Jonathan.

JENNY: I must say, Mr. Jessamy, if he copies after me, he will be vastly, monstrously polite.

JESSAMY: Stay here one moment, and I will call him.—[*Calls.*] Jonathan!—Mr. Jonathan!—

JONATHAN [*within*]: Holla! there.—[*Enters.*] You promise to stand by me—six bows you say. [*Bows.*]

JESSAMY: Mrs. Jenny,[33] I have the honour of presenting Mr. Jonathan, Colonel Manly's waiter, to you. I am extremely happy that I have it in my power to make two worthy people acquainted with each other's merits.

JENNY: So, Mr. Jonathan, I hear you were at the play last night.

JONATHAN: At the play! why, did you think I went to the devil's drawing-room?

---

[32] "Young Stanhope" was Philip Stanhope (1732–1768), illegitimate son of the Earl of Chesterfield and Elizabeth du Bouchet.

[33] "Mrs.," like "Mistress," was an honorific applied to unmarried gentlewomen, as well as to wives, in eighteenth-century America. Here, Jessamy flatters Jenny, who is neither married nor of high social rank.

JENNY: The devil's drawing-room!

JONATHAN: Yes; why an't cards and dice the devil's device, and the play-house the shop where the devil hangs out the vanities of the world upon the tenter-hooks of temptation? I believe you have not heard how they were acting the old boy one night, and the wicked one came among them sure enough, and went right off in a storm, and carried one quarter of the play-house with him. Oh! no, no, no! you won't catch me at a play-house, I warrant you.

JENNY: Well, Mr. Jonathan, though I don't scruple your veracity, I have some reasons for believing you were there: pray, where were you about six o'clock?

JONATHAN: Why, I went to see one Mr. Morrison, the *hocus pocus* man; they said as how he could eat a case knife.

JENNY: Well, and how did you find the place?

JONATHAN: As I was going about here and there, to and again, to find it, I saw a great crowd of folks going into a long entry that had lanthernes over the door; so I asked a man whether that was not the place where they played *hocus pocus*? He was a very civil, kind man, though he did speak like the Hessians;[34] he lifted up his eyes and said, "They play *hocus pocus* tricks enough there, Got knows, mine friend."

JENNY: Well—

JONATHAN: So I went right in, and they shewed me away, clean up to the garret, just like meeting-house gallery. And so I saw a power of topping folks, all sitting round in little cabbins, "just like father's corn-cribs"; and then there was such a squeaking with the fiddles, and such a tarnal blaze with the lights, my head was near turned. At last the people that sat near me set up such a hissing—hiss—like so many mad cats; and then they went thump, thump, thump, just like our Peleg threshing wheat, and stampt away, just like the nation; and called out for one Mr. Langolee,[35]—I suppose he helps act the tricks.

JENNY: Well, and what did you do all this time?

JONATHAN: Gor,[36] I—I liked the fun, and so I thumpt away, and hiss'd as lustily as the best of 'em. One sailor-looking man that sat by me, seeing me stamp, and knowing I was a cute fellow, because I could

---

[34] Hessians: German soldiers employed by the British during the American Revolution.

[35] "Old Langolee" was a popular Irish song.

[36] Gor: a mild oath, used to express surprise or disbelief.

make a roaring noise, clapt me on the shoulder and said, "You are a
d——d hearty cock, smite my timbers!" I told him so I was, but I
thought he need not swear so, and make use of such naughty words.

JESSAMY: The savage!—Well, and did you see the man with his tricks?

JONATHAN: Why, I vow, as I was looking out for him, they lifted up a
great green cloth and let us look right into the next neighbor's house.
Have you a good many houses in New-York made so in that 'ere way?

JENNY: Not many; but did you see the family?

JONATHAN: Yes, swamp it; I see'd the family.

JENNY: Well, and how did you like them?

JONATHAN: Why, I vow they were pretty much like other families;—
there was a poor, good-natured, curse of a husband, and a sad rantipole[37] of a wife.

JENNY: But did you see no other folks?

JONATHAN: Yes. There was one youngster; they called him Mr. Joseph;
he talked as sober and as pious as a minister; but, like some ministers
that I know, he was a sly tike in his heart for all that. He was going
to ask a young woman to spark it with him, and—the Lord have
mercy on my soul!—she was another man's wife.

JESSAMY: The Wabash!

JENNY: And did you see any more folks?

JONATHAN: Why, they came on as thick as mustard. For my part, I
thought the house was haunted. There was a soldier fellow, who
talked about his row de dow, dow, and courted a young woman; but,
of all the cute folk I saw, I liked one little fellow—

JENNY: Aye! who was he?

JONATHAN: Why, he had red hair, and a little round plump face like
mine, only not altogether so handsome. His name was—Darby;—
that was his baptizing name; his other name I forgot. Oh! it was
Wig—Wag—Wag-all, Darby Wag-all,[38]—pray, do you know him?—
I should like to take a sling with him, or a drap of cyder with a pep-
per-pod in it, to make it warm and comfortable.

JENNY: I can't say I have that pleasure.

---

[37] Rantipole: an ill-behaved person.

[38] Actor Thomas Wignell, who played Jonathan in *The Contrast,* often played the role
of Darby in John O'Keefe's popular comic opera *The Poor Soldier.* One of his performances, which Tyler probably witnessed, was at the John Street Theatre in New York in
March 1787 (Jeffrey H. Richards, *Drama, Theatre, and Identity in the American New Republic* [Cambridge, Eng.: Cambridge University Press, 2005], 61).

JONATHAN: I wish you did; he is a cute fellow. But there was one thing I didn't like in that Mr. Darby; and that was, he was afraid of some of them 'ere shooting irons, such as your troopers wear on training days. Now, I'm a true born Yankee American son of liberty, and I never was afraid of a gun yet in all my life.

JENNY: Well, Mr. Jonathan, you were certainly at the play-house.

JONATHAN: I at the play-house!—Why didn't I see the play then?

JENNY: Why, the people you saw were players.

JONATHAN: Mercy on my soul! did I see the wicked players?—Mayhap that 'ere Darby that I liked so was the old serpent himself, and had his cloven foot in his pocket. Why, I vow, now I come to think on't, the candles seemed to burn blue, and I am sure where I sat it smelt tarnally of brimstone.

JESSAMY: Well, Mr. Jonathan, from your account, which I confess is very accurate, you must have been at the play-house.

JONATHAN: Why, I vow, I began to smell a rat. When I came away, I went to the man for my money again; you want your money? says he; yes, says I; for what? says he; why, says I, no man shall jocky me out of my money; I paid my money to see sights, and the dogs a bit of a sight have I seen, unless you call listening to people's private business a sight. Why, says he, it is the School for Scandalization.—The School for Scandalization![39]—Oh! ho! no wonder you New-York folks are so cute at it, when you go to school to learn it; and so I jogged off.

JESSAMY: My dear Jenny, my master's business drags me from you; would to heaven I knew no other servitude than to your charms.

JONATHAN: Well, but don't go; you won't leave me so—

JESSAMY: Excuse me.—[*Aside to him.*] Remember the cash.

   Exit.]

JENNY: Mr. Jonathan, won't you please to sit down? Mr. Jessamy tells me you wanted to have some conversation with me.

   [*Having brought forward two chairs, they sit.*]

---

[39] Richard Brinsley Sheridan's *The School for Scandal* was performed in New York on 21 March 1787. Thomas Wignell played the role of Joseph Surface in that production (Tanselle, *Royall Tyler*, 50; Kenneth Silverman, *A Cultural History of the American Revolution* [New York: Crowell, 1976], 541).

JONATHAN: Ma'am!—

JENNY: Sir!—

JONATHAN: Ma'am!—

JENNY: Pray, how do you like the city, Sir?

JONATHAN: Ma'am!—

JENNY: I say, Sir, how do you like New-York?

JONATHAN: Ma'am!—

JENNY: The stupid creature! but I must pass some little time with him, if it is only to endeavour to learn whether it was his master that made such an abrupt entrance into our house, and my young mistress's heart, this morning. As you don't seem to like to talk, Mr. Jonathan —do you sing?

JONATHAN: Gor, I—I am glad she asked that, for I forgot what Mr. Jessamy bid me say, and I dare as well be hanged as act what he bid me do, I'm so ashamed. [*Aside.*] Yes, Ma'am, I can sing—I can sing Mear, Old Hundred, and Bangor.[40]

JENNY: Oh! I don't mean psalm tunes. Have you no little song to please the ladies, such as Roslin Castle, or the Maid of the Mill?

JONATHAN: Why, all my tunes go to meeting tunes, save one, and I count you won't altogether like that 'ere.

JENNY: What is it called?

JONATHAN: I am sure you have heard folks talk about it; it is called Yankee Doodle.

JENNY: Oh! it is the tune I am fond of; and if I know anything of my mistress, she would be glad to dance to it. Pray, sing!

JONATHAN [*Sings.*]:

> Father and I went up to camp,
> Along with Captain Goodwin;
> And there we saw the men and boys,
> As thick as hasty-pudding.
> Yankee doodle do, etc.
>
> And there we saw a swamping gun,
> Big as log of maple,
> On a little deuced cart,
> A load for father's cattle.
> Yankee doodle do, etc.

[40] "Mear," "Old Hundred," and "Bangor" are hymns.

> And every time they fired it off
> It took a horn of powder,
> It made a noise—like father's gun,
> Only a nation louder.
> Yankee doodle do, etc.
>
> There was a man in our town,
> His name was—

No, no, that won't do. Now, if I was with Tabitha Wymen and Jemima Cawley down at father Chase's, I shouldn't mind singing this all out before them—you would be affronted if I was to sing that, though that's a lucky thought; if you should be affronted, I have something dang'd cute, which Jessamy told me to say to you.

JENNY: Is that all! I assure you I like it of all things.

JONATHAN: No, no; I can sing more; some other time, when you and I are better acquainted, I'll sing the whole of it—no, no—that's a fib—I can't sing but a hundred and ninety verses; our Tabitha at home can sing it all.—[*Sings.*]

> Marblehead's a rocky place,
> And Cape-Cod is sandy;
> Charlestown is burnt down,
> Boston is the dandy.
> Yankee doodle, doodle do, etc.

I vow, my own town song has put me into such topping spirits that I believe I'll begin to do a little, as Jessamy says we must when we go a-courting.—[*Runs and kisses her.*] Burning rivers! cooling flames! red-hot roses! pig-nuts! hasty-pudding and ambrosia!

JENNY: What means this freedom? you insulting wretch. [*Strikes him.*]

JONATHAN: Are you affronted?

JENNY: Affronted! with what looks shall I express my anger?

JONATHAN: Looks! why as to the matter of looks, you look as cross as a witch.

JENNY: Have you no feeling for the delicacy of my sex?

JONATHAN: Feeling! Gor, I—I feel the delicacy of your sex pretty smartly [*rubbing his cheek*], though, I vow, I thought when you city ladies courted and married, and all that, you put feeling out of the question. But I want to know whether you are really affronted, or only pretend to be so? 'Cause, if you are certainly right down affronted, I am at the end of my tether; Jessamy didn't tell me what to say to you.

JENNY: Pretend to be affronted!

JONATHAN: Aye, aye, if you only pretend, you shall hear how I'll go to work to make cherubim consequences. [*Runs up to her.*]

JENNY: Begone, you brute!

JONATHAN: That looks like mad; but I won't lose my speech. My dearest Jenny—your name is Jenny, I think?—My dearest Jenny, though I have the highest esteem for the sweet favours you have just now granted me—Gor, that's a fib, though; but Jessamy says it is not wicked to tell lies to the women. [*Aside.*] I say, though I have the highest esteem for the favours you have just now granted me, yet you will consider that, as soon as the dissolvable knot is tied, they will no longer be favours, but only matters of duty and matters of course.

JENNY: Marry you! you audacious monster! get out of my sight, or, rather, let me fly from you.

[*Exit hastily.*]

JONATHAN: Gor! she's gone off in a swinging passion, before I had time to think of consequences. If this is the way with your city ladies, give me the twenty acres of rock, the Bible, the cow, and Tabitha, and a little peaceable bundling.[41]

SCENE II.

The Mall.

Enter MANLY: It must be so, Montague! and it is not all the tribe of Mandevilles[42] that shall convince me that a nation, to become great, must first become dissipated. Luxury is surely the bane of a nation: Luxury! which enervates both soul and body, by opening a thousand new sources of enjoyment, opens, also, a thousand new sources of

[41] Bundling: the New England custom of a courting couple sharing a bed without undressing.

[42] Bernard Mandeville was the author of *The Fable of the Bees* (1714), in which he defended luxury and maintained that private vices (and more generally the pursuit of self-interest) could engender social progress.

contention and want: Luxury! which renders a people weak at home, and accessible to bribery, corruption, and force from abroad. When the Grecian states knew no other tools than the axe and the saw, the Grecians were a great, a free, and a happy people. The kings of Greece devoted their lives to the service of their country, and her senators knew no other superiority over their fellow-citizens than a glorious pre-eminence in danger and virtue. They exhibited to the world a noble spectacle,—a number of independent states united by a similarity of language, sentiment, manners, common interest, and common consent, in one grand mutual league of protection. And, thus united, long might they have continued the cherishers of arts and sciences, the protectors of the oppressed, the scourge of tyrants, and the safe asylum of liberty. But when foreign gold, and still more pernicious foreign luxury, had crept among them, they sapped the vitals of their virtue. The virtues of their ancestors were only found in their writings. Envy and suspicion, the vices of little minds, possessed them. The various states engendered jealousies of each other; and, more unfortunately, growing jealous of their great federal council, the Amphictyons, they forgot that their common safety had existed, and would exist, in giving them an honourable extensive prerogative. The common good was lost in the pursuit of private interest; and that people who, by uniting, might have stood against the world in arms, by dividing, crumbled into ruin;—their name is now only known in the page of the historian, and what they once were is all we have left to admire. Oh! that America! Oh! that my country, would, in this her day, learn the things which belong to her peace!

Enter DIMPLE.

DIMPLE: You are Colonel Manly, I presume?
MANLY: At your service, Sir.
DIMPLE: My name is Dimple, Sir. I have the honour to be a lodger in the same house with you, and, hearing you were in the Mall, came hither to take the liberty of joining you.
MANLY: You are very obliging, Sir.
DIMPLE: As I understand you are a stranger here, Sir, I have taken the liberty to introduce myself to your acquaintance, as possibly I may have it in my power to point out some things in this city worthy your notice.

MANLY: An attention to strangers is worthy a liberal mind, and must ever be gratefully received. But to a soldier, who has no fixed abode, such attentions are particularly pleasing.

DIMPLE: Sir, there is no character so respectable as that of a soldier. And, indeed, when we reflect how much we owe to those brave men who have suffered so much in the service of their country, and secured to us those inestimable blessings that we now enjoy, our liberty and independence, they demand every attention which gratitude can pay. For my own part, I never meet an officer, but I embrace him as my friend, nor a private in distress, but I insensibly extend my charity to him.—[*Aside*] I have hit the Bumkin off very tolerably.

MANLY: Give me your hand, Sir! I do not proffer this hand to everybody; but you steal into my heart. I hope I am as insensible to flattery as most men; but I declare (it may be my weak side) that I never hear the name of soldier mentioned with respect, but I experience a thrill of pleasure which I never feel on any other occasion.

DIMPLE: Will you give me leave, my dear Colonel, to confer an obligation on myself, by shewing you some civilities during your stay here, and giving a similar opportunity to some of my friends?

MANLY: Sir, I thank you; but I believe my stay in this city will be very short.

DIMPLE: I can introduce you to some men of excellent sense, in whose company you will esteem yourself happy; and, by way of amusement, to some fine girls, who will listen to your soft things with pleasure.

MANLY: Sir, I should be proud of the honour of being acquainted with those gentlemen;—but, as for the ladies, I don't understand you.

DIMPLE: Why, Sir, I need not tell you, that when a young gentleman is alone with a young lady he must say some soft things to her fair cheek—indeed, the lady will expect it. To be sure, there is not much pleasure when a man of the world and a finished coquette meet, who perfectly know each other; but how delicious is it to excite the emotions of joy, hope, expectation, and delight in the bosom of a lovely girl who believes every tittle of what you say to be serious!

MANLY: Serious, Sir! In my opinion, the man who, under pretensions of marriage, can plant thorns in the bosom of an innocent, unsuspecting girl is more detestable than a common robber, in the same proportion as private violence is more despicable than open force, and money of less value than happiness.

DIMPLE: How he awes me by the superiority of his sentiments. [*Aside.*]

As you say, Sir, a gentleman should be cautious how he mentions marriage.

MANLY: Cautious, Sir! No person more approves of an intercourse between the sexes than I do. Female conversation softens our manners, whilst our discourse, from the superiority of our literary advantages, improves their minds. But, in our young country, where there is no such thing as gallantry, when a gentleman speaks of love to a lady, whether he mentions marriage or not, she ought to conclude either that he meant to insult her or that his intentions are the most serious and honourable. How mean, how cruel, is it, by a thousand tender assiduities, to win the affections of an amiable girl, and, though you leave her virtue unspotted, to betray her into the appearance of so many tender partialities, that every man of delicacy would suppress his inclination towards her, by supposing her heart engaged! Can any man, for the trivial gratification of his leisure hours, affect the happiness of a whole life! His not having spoken of marriage may add to his perfidy, but can be no excuse for his conduct.

DIMPLE: Sir, I admire your sentiments;—they are mine. The light observations that fell from me were only a principle of the tongue; they came not from the heart; my practice has ever disapproved these principles.

MANLY: I believe you, Sir. I should with reluctance suppose that those pernicious sentiments could find admittance into the heart of a gentleman.

DIMPLE: I am now, Sir, going to visit a family, where, if you please, I will have the honour of introducing you. Mr. Manly's ward, Miss Letitia, is a young lady of immense fortune; and his niece, Miss Charlotte Manly, is a young lady of great sprightliness and beauty.

MANLY: That gentleman, Sir, is my uncle, and Miss Manly my sister.

DIMPLE: The devil she is! [*Aside.*] Miss Manly your sister, Sir? I rejoice to hear it, and feel a double pleasure in being known to you.—Plague on him! I wish he was at Boston again, with all my soul. [*Aside.*]

MANLY: Come, Sir, will you go?

DIMPLE: I will follow you in a moment, Sir.

[*Exit* MANLY.]

DIMPLE: Plague on it! this is unlucky. A fighting brother is a cursed appendage to a fine girl. Egad! I just stopped in time; had he not discovered himself, in two minutes more I should have told him how well I was with his sister. Indeed, I cannot see the satisfaction of an intrigue, if one can't have the pleasure of communicating it to our friends.

[*Exit.*

End of the Third Act.

Act IV.

SCENE I.

CHARLOTTE's *Apartment.*

CHARLOTTE *leading in* MARIA.

CHARLOTTE: This is so kind, my sweet friend, to come to see me at this moment. I declare, if I were going to be married in a few days, as you are, I should scarce have found time to visit my friends.

MARIA: Do you think, then, that there is an impropriety in it?—How should you dispose of your time?

CHARLOTTE: Why, I should be shut up in my chamber; and my head would so run upon—upon—upon the solemn ceremony that I was to pass through!—I declare, it would take me above two hours merely to learn that little monosyllable—*Yes.* Ah! my dear, your sentimental imagination does not conceive what that little tiny word implies.

MARIA: Spare me your raillery, my sweet friend; I should love your agreeable vivacity at any other time.

CHARLOTTE: Why, this is the very time to amuse you. You grieve me to see you look so unhappy.

MARIA: Have I not reason to look so?

CHARLOTTE: What new grief distresses you?

MARIA: Oh! how sweet it is, when the heart is borne down with misfortune, to recline and repose on the bosom of friendship! Heaven knows that, although it is improper for a young lady to praise a gentleman, yet I have ever concealed Mr. Dimple's foibles, and spoke of him as of one whose reputation I expected would be linked with mine; but his late conduct towards me has turned my coolness into contempt. He behaves as if he meant to insult and disgust me; whilst my father, in the last conversation on the subject of our marriage, spoke of it as a matter which lay near his heart, and in which he would not bear contradiction.

CHARLOTTE: This works well; oh! the generous Dimple. I'll endeavour to excite her to discharge him. [*Aside.*] But, my dear friend, your happiness depends on yourself. Why don't you discard him? Though the match has been of long standing, I would not be forced to make myself miserable: no parent in the world should oblige me to marry the man I did not like.

MARIA: Oh! my dear, you never lived with your parents, and do not know what influence a father's frowns have upon a daughter's heart. Besides, what have I to alledge against Mr. Dimple, to justify myself to the world? He carries himself so smoothly, that every one would impute the blame to me, and call me capricious.

CHARLOTTE: And call her capricious! Did ever such an objection start into the heart of woman? For my part, I wish I had fifty lovers to discard, for no other reason than because I did not fancy them. My dear Maria, you will forgive me; I know your candour and confidence in me; but I have at times, I confess, been led to suppose that some other gentleman was the cause of your aversion to Mr. Dimple.

MARIA: No, my sweet friend, you may be assured, that though I have seen many gentlemen I could prefer to Mr. Dimple, yet I never saw one that I thought I could give my hand to, until this morning.

CHARLOTTE: This morning!

MARIA: Yes; one of the strangest accidents in the world. The odious Dimple, after disgusting me with his conversation, had just left me, when a gentleman, who, it seems, boards in the same house with him, saw him coming out of our door, and, the houses looking very much alike, he came into our house instead of his lodgings; nor did he discover his mistake until he got into the parlour, where I was; he then bowed so gracefully, made such a genteel apology, and looked so manly and noble!—

CHARLOTTE [*aside*]: I see some folks, though it is so great an impropriety, can praise a gentleman, when he happens to be the man of their fancy.

MARIA: I don't know how it was,—I hope he did not think me indelicate,—but I asked him, I believe, to sit down, or pointed to a chair. He sat down, and, instead of having recourse to observations upon the weather, or hackneyed criticisms upon the theatre, he entered readily into a conversation worthy a man of sense to speak, and a lady of delicacy and sentiment to hear. He was not strictly handsome, but he spoke the language of sentiment, and his eyes looked tenderness and honour.

CHARLOTTE: Oh! [*eagerly*] you sentimental, grave girls, when your hearts are once touched, beat us rattles a bar's length. And so you are quite in love with this he-angel?

MARIA: In love with him! How can you rattle so, Charlotte? am I not going to be miserable? [*Sighs.*] In love with a gentleman I never saw but one hour in my life, and don't know his name! No; I only wished that the man I shall marry may look, and talk, and act, just like him. Besides, my dear, he is a married man.

CHARLOTTE: Why, that was good-natured—he told you so, I suppose, in mere charity, to prevent you falling in love with him?

MARIA: He didn't tell me so; [*peevishly*] he looked as if he was married.

CHARLOTTE: How, my dear, did he look sheepish?

MARIA: I am sure he has a susceptible heart, and the ladies of his acquaintance must be very stupid not to—

CHARLOTTE: Hush! I hear some person coming.

Enter LETITIA.

LETITIA: My dear Maria, I am happy to see you. Lud! what a pity it is that you have purchased your wedding clothes.

MARIA: I think so. [*Sighing.*]

LETITIA: Why, my dear, there is the sweetest parcel of silks come over you ever saw! Nancy Brilliant has a full suit come; she sent over her measure, and it fits her to a hair; it is immensely dressy, and made for a court-hoop. I thought they said the large hoops were going out of fashion.

CHARLOTTE: Did you see the hat? Is it a fact that the deep laces round the border is still the fashion?

DIMPLE [*within*]: Upon my honour, Sir.

MARIA: Ha! Dimple's voice! My dear, I must take leave of you. There are some things necessary to be done at our house. Can't I go through the other room?

Enter DIMPLE *and* MANLY.

DIMPLE: Ladies, your most obedient.

CHARLOTTE: Miss Van Rough, shall I present my brother Henry to you? Colonel Manly, Maria,—Miss Van Rough, brother.

MARIA: Her brother! [*Turns and sees Manly.*] Oh! my heart! the very gentleman I have been praising.

MANLY: The same amiable girl I saw this morning!

CHARLOTTE: Why, you look as if you were acquainted.

MANLY: I unintentionally intruded into this lady's presence this morning, for which she was so good as to promise me her forgiveness.

CHARLOTTE [*aside*]: Oh! ho! is that the case! Have these two pensero-
sos been together? Were they Henry's eyes that looked so tenderly?
[*Whispering loud to Maria.*] And so you promised to pardon him?
and could you be so good-natured? have you really forgiven him? I
beg you would do it for my sake. But, my dear, as you are in such
haste, it would be cruel to detain you; I can show you the way
through the other room.

MARIA: Spare me, my sprightly friend.

MANLY: The lady does not, I hope, intend to deprive us of the pleasure
of her company so soon.

CHARLOTTE: She has only a mantua-maker who waits for her at home.
But, as I am to give my opinion of the dress, I think she cannot go
yet. We were talking of the fashions when you came in, but I suppose
the subject must be changed to something of more importance now.
Mr. Dimple, will you favour us with an account of the public enter-
tainments?

DIMPLE: Why, really, Miss Manly, you could not have asked me a question more *mal-apropos*. For my part, I must confess that, to a man
who has travelled, there is nothing that is worthy the name of amusement to be found in this city.

CHARLOTTE: Except visiting the ladies.

DIMPLE: Pardon me, Madam; that is the avocation of a man of taste.
But for amusement, I positively know of nothing that can be called
so, unless you dignify with that title the hopping once a fortnight to
the sound of two or three squeaking fiddles, and the clattering of the
old tavern windows, or sitting to see the miserable mummers, whom
you call actors, murder comedy and make a farce of tragedy.

MANLY: Do you never attend the theatre, Sir?

DIMPLE: I was tortured there once.

CHARLOTTE: Pray, Mr. Dimple, was it a tragedy or a comedy?

DIMPLE: Faith, Madam, I cannot tell; for I sat with my back to the stage
all the time, admiring a much better actress than any there—a lady
who played the fine woman to perfection; though, by the laugh of the
horrid creatures round me, I suppose it was comedy. Yet, on second
thoughts, it might be some hero in a tragedy, dying so comically as to
set the whole house in an uproar. Colonel, I presume you have been
in Europe?

MANLY: Indeed, Sir, I was never ten leagues from the continent.

DIMPLE: Believe me, Colonel, you have an immense pleasure to come;

and when you shall have seen the brilliant exhibitions of Europe, you will learn to despise the amusements of this country as much as I do.

MANLY: Therefore I do not wish to see them; for I can never esteem that knowledge valuable which tends to give me a distaste for my native country.

DIMPLE: Well, Colonel, though you have not travelled, you have read.

MANLY: I have, a little; and by it have discovered that there is a laudable partiality which ignorant, untravelled men entertain for everything that belongs to their native country. I call it laudable; it injures no one; adds to their own happiness; and, when extended, becomes the noble principle of patriotism. Travelled gentlemen rise superior, in their own opinion, to this; but if the contempt which they contract for their country is the most valuable acquisition of their travels, I am far from thinking that their time and money are well spent.

MARIA: What noble sentiments!

CHARLOTTE: Let my brother set out where he will in the fields of conversation, he is sure to end his tour in the temple of gravity.

MANLY: Forgive me, my sister. I love my country; it has its foibles undoubtedly;—some foreigners will with pleasure remark them—but such remarks fall very ungracefully from the lips of her citizens.

DIMPLE: You are perfectly in the right, Colonel—America has her faults.

MANLY: Yes, Sir; and we, her children, should blush for them in private, and endeavour, as individuals, to reform them. But, if our country has its errors in common with other countries, I am proud to say America—I mean the United States—has displayed virtues and achievements which modern nations may admire, but of which they have seldom set us the example.

CHARLOTTE: But, brother, we must introduce you to some of our gay folks, and let you see the city, such as it is. Mr. Dimple is known to almost every family in town; he will doubtless take a pleasure in introducing you.

DIMPLE: I shall esteem every service I can render your brother an honour.

MANLY: I fear the business I am upon will take up all my time, and my family will be anxious to hear from me.

MARIA: His family! but what is it to me that he is married! [*Aside.*] Pray, how did you leave your lady, Sir?

CHARLOTTE: My brother is not married [*observing her anxiety*]; it is only an odd way he has of expressing himself. Pray, brother, is this business, which you make your continual excuse, a secret?

MANLY: No, sister; I came hither to solicit the honourable Congress, that a number of my brave old soldiers may be put upon the pension-list, who were, at first, not judged to be so materially wounded as to need the public assistance. My sister says true [*to Maria*]: I call my late soldiers my family. Those who were not in the field in the late glorious contest, and those who were, have their respective merits; but, I confess, my old brother-soldiers are dearer to me than the former description. Friendships made in adversity are lasting; our countrymen may forget us, but that is no reason why we should forget one another. But I must leave you; my time of engagement approaches.

CHARLOTTE: Well, but, brother, if you will go, will you please to conduct my fair friend home? You live in the same street—I was to have gone with her myself—[*Aside.*] A lucky thought.

MARIA: I am obliged to your sister, Sir, and was just intending to go.

[*Going.*]

MANLY: I shall attend her with pleasure.

[*Exit with* MARIA, *followed by* DIMPLE *and* CHARLOTTE.]

MARIA: Now, pray, don't betray me to your brother.

CHARLOTTE [*just as she* sees *him make a motion to take his leave*]: One word with you, brother, if you please.

[*Follows them out.*
Manent,[43] DIMPLE *and* LETITIA.

DIMPLE: You received the billet I sent you, I presume?

LETITIA: Hush!—Yes.

DIMPLE: When shall I pay my respects to you?

LETITIA: At eight I shall be unengaged.

Reënter CHARLOTTE.

DIMPLE [*to Charlotte*]: Did my lovely angel receive my billet?

CHARLOTTE: Yes.

---

[43] *Manent*: they remain.

DIMPLE: What hour shall I expect with impatience?

CHARLOTTE: At eight I shall be at home unengaged.

DIMPLE: Unfortunate! I have a horrid engagement of business at that hour. Can't you finish your visit earlier and let six be the happy hour?

CHARLOTTE: You know your influence over me.

[*Exeunt severally.*

SCENE II.

VAN ROUGH'S *House.*

VAN ROUGH, *alone:* It cannot possibly be true! The son of my old friend can't have acted so unadvisedly. Seventeen thousand pounds! in bills! Mr. Transfer must have been mistaken. He always appeared so prudent, and talked so well upon money matters, and even assured me that he intended to change his dress for a suit of clothes which would not cost so much, and look more substantial, as soon as he married. No, no, no! it can't be; it cannot be. But, however, I must look out sharp. I did not care what his principles or his actions were, so long as he minded the main chance. Seventeen thousand pounds! If he had lost it in trade, why the best men may have ill-luck; but to game it away, as Transfer says—why, at this rate, his whole estate may go in one night, and, what is ten times worse, mine into the bargain.[44] No, no; Mary is right. Leave women to look out in these matters; for all they look as if they didn't know a journal from a ledger, when their interest is concerned they know what's what; they mind the main chance as well as the best of us. I wonder Mary did not tell me she knew of his spending his money so foolishly. Seventeen thousand pounds! Why, if my daughter was standing up to be married, I would forbid the banns, if I found it was to a man who did not mind the main chance.—Hush! I hear somebody coming. 'Tis Mary's voice; a man with her too! I shouldn't be surprised if this should be the other string to her bow. Aye, aye, let them alone; women understand the main chance.—Though, i' faith, I'll listen a little.

---

[44] Under the common law doctrine of coverture, a husband controlled his wife's property. Because Maria stood to inherit her father's entire estate, Van Rough's property would fall into the hands of her prospective husband, Dimple, who be forced to liquidate it to pay his debts.

[*Retires into a closet.*
MANLY *leading in* MARIA.

MANLY: I hope you will excuse my speaking upon so important a subject so abruptly; but, the moment I entered your room, you struck me as the lady whom I had long loved in imagination, and never hoped to see.

MARIA: Indeed, Sir, I have been led to hear more upon this subject than I ought.

MANLY: Do you, then, disapprove my suit, Madam, or the abruptness of my introducing it? If the latter, my peculiar situation, being obliged to leave the city in a few days, will, I hope, be my excuse; if the former, I will retire, for I am sure I would not give a moment's inquietude to her whom I could devote my life to please. I am not so indelicate as to seek your immediate approbation; permit me only to be near you, and by a thousand tender assiduities to endeavour to excite a grateful return.

MARIA: I have a father, whom I would die to make happy; he will disapprove—

MANLY: Do you think me so ungenerous as to seek a place in your esteem without his consent? You must—you ever ought to consider that man as unworthy of you who seeks an interest in your heart contrary to a father's approbation. A young lady should reflect that the loss of a lover may be supplied, but nothing can compensate for the loss of a parent's affection. Yet, why do you suppose your father would disapprove? In our country, the affections are not sacrificed to riches or family aggrandizement: should you approve, my family is decent, and my rank honourable.

MARIA: You distress me, Sir.

MANLY: Then I will sincerely beg your excuse for obtruding so disagreeable a subject, and retire.

[*Going.*]

MARIA: Stay, Sir! your generosity and good opinion of me deserve a return; but why must I declare what, for these few hours, I have scarce suffered myself to think?—I am—

MANLY: What?

MARIA: Engaged, Sir; and, in a few days, to be married to the gentleman you saw at your sister's.

MANLY: Engaged to be married! And have I been basely invading the rights of another? Why have you permitted this? Is this the return for the partiality I declared for you?

MARIA: You distress me, Sir. What would you have me say? You are too generous to wish the truth. Ought I to say that I dared not suffer myself to think of my engagement, and that I am going to give my hand without my heart? Would you have me confess a partiality for you? If so, your triumph is compleat, and can be only more so when days of misery with the man I cannot love will make me think of him whom I could prefer.

MANLY [*after a pause*]: We are both unhappy; but it is your duty to obey your parent—mine to obey my honour. Let us, therefore, both follow the path of rectitude; and of this we may be assured, that if we are not happy, we shall, at least, deserve to be so. Adieu! I dare not trust myself longer with you.

[*Exeunt severally.*

End of the Fourth Act.

Act V.

SCENE I.

DIMPLE's *Lodgings.*

JESSAMY *meeting* JONATHAN.

JESSAMY: Well, Mr. Jonathan, what success with the fair?

JONATHAN: Why, such a tarnal cross tike you never saw! You would have counted she had lived upon crab-apples and vinegar for a fortnight. But what the rattle makes you look so tarnation glum?

JESSAMY: I was thinking, Mr. Jonathan, what could be the reason of her carrying herself so coolly to you.

JONATHAN: Coolly, do you call it? Why, I vow, she was fire-hot angry: may be it was because I buss'd her.

JESSAMY: No, no, Mr. Jonathan; there must be some other cause; I never yet knew a lady angry at being kissed.

JONATHAN: Well, if it is not the young woman's bashfulness, I vow I can't conceive why she shouldn't like me.

JESSAMY: May be it is because you have not the Graces, Mr. Jonathan.

JONATHAN: Grace! Why, does the young woman expect I must be converted before I court her?

JESSAMY: I mean graces of person: for instance, my lord tells us that we must cut off our nails even at top, in small segments of circles—though you won't understand that; in the next place, you must regulate your laugh.

JONATHAN: Maple-log seize it! don't I laugh natural?

JESSAMY: That's the very fault, Mr. Jonathan. Besides, you absolutely misplace it. I was told by a friend of mine that you laughed outright at the play the other night, when you ought only to have tittered.

JONATHAN: Gor! I—what does one go to see fun for if they can't laugh?

JESSAMY: You may laugh; but you must laugh by rule.

JONATHAN: Swamp it—laugh by rule! Well, I should like that tarnally.

JESSAMY: Why, you know, Mr. Jonathan, that to dance, a lady to play with her fan, or a gentleman with his cane, and all other natural motions, are regulated by art. My master has composed an immensely pretty gamut, by which any lady or gentleman, with a few years' close application, may learn to laugh as gracefully as if they were born and bred to it.

JONATHAN: Mercy on my soul! A gamut for laughing—just like fa, la, sol?

JESSAMY: Yes. It comprises every possible display of jocularity, from an *affettuoso* smile to a *piano* titter, or full chorus *fortissimo* ha, ha, ha![45] My master employs his leisure hours in marking out the plays, like a cathedral chanting-book, that the ignorant may know where to laugh; and that pit, box, and gallery may keep time together, and not have a snigger in one part of the house, a broad grin in the other, and a d——d grum look in the third. How delightful to see the audience all smile together, then look on their books, then twist their mouths into an agreeable simper, then altogether shake the house with a general ha, ha, ha! loud as a full chorus of Handel's at an Abbey commemoration.[46]

JONATHAN: Ha, ha, ha! that's dang'd cute, I swear.

JESSAMY: The gentlemen, you see, will laugh the tenor; the ladies will play the counter-tenor; the beaux will squeak the treble; and our jolly friends in the gallery a thorough base, ho, ho, ho!

JONATHAN: Well, can't you let me see that gamut?

JESSAMY: Oh! yes, Mr. Jonathan; here it is. [*Takes out a book.*] Oh! no, this is only a titter with its variations. Ah, here it is. [*Takes out another.*] Now, you must know, Mr. Jonathan, this is a piece written by Ben Johnson,[47] which I have set to my master's gamut. The places where you must smile, look grave, or laugh outright, are marked below the line. Now look over me. "There was a certain man"—now you must smile.

JONATHAN: Well, read it again; I warrant I'll mind my eye.

JESSAMY: "There was a certain man, who had a sad scolding wife,"—now you must laugh.

JONATHAN: Tarnation! That's no laughing matter though.

JESSAMY: "And she lay sick a-dying";—now you must titter.

[45] *Affettuoso:* with feeling; *piano:* softly or quietly; *fortissimo:* loudly.

[46] George Frederic Handel (1685–1759), the most important composer in eighteenth-century England, wrote several anthems used in royal ceremonies, such as coronations, which took place in Westminster Abbey.

[47] Possibly the English poet Ben Jonson (1572–1637), though Jonson was not the author of the passage Jessamy reads.

JONATHAN: What, snigger when the good woman's a-dying! Gor, I—

JESSAMY: Yes, the notes say you must—"and she asked her husband leave to make a will,"—now you must begin to look grave;—"and her husband said"—

JONATHAN: Ay, what did her husband say? Something dang'd cute, I reckon.

JESSAMY: "And her husband said, you have had your will all your life-time, and would you have it after you are dead, too?"

JONATHAN: Ho, ho, ho! There the old man was even with her; he was up to the notch—ha, ha, ha!

JESSAMY: But, Mr. Jonathan, you must not laugh so. Why you ought to have tittered *piano,* and you have laughed *fortissimo.* Look here; you see these marks, A, B, C, and so on; these are the references to the other part of the book. Let us turn to it, and you will see the direc-tions how to manage the muscles. This [*turns over*] was note D you blundered at.—You must purse the mouth into a smile, then titter, discovering the lower part of the three front upper teeth.

JONATHAN: How? read it again.

JESSAMY: "There was a certain man"—very well!—"who had a sad scolding wife,"—why don't you laugh?

JONATHAN: Now, that scolding wife sticks in my gizzard so pluckily that I can't laugh for the blood and nowns of me. Let me look grave here, and I'll laugh your belly full, where the old creature's a-dying.

JESSAMY: "And she asked her husband"—[*Bell rings.*] My master's bell! he's returned, I fear.—Here, Mr. Jonathan, take this gamut; and I make no doubt but with a few years' close application, you may be able to smile gracefully."

[*Exeunt severally.*

SCENE II.

CHARLOTTE's *Apartment.*

Enter MANLY.

MANLY: What, no one at home? How unfortunate to meet the only lady my heart was ever moved by, to find her engaged to another, and confessing her partiality for me! Yet engaged to a man who, by her intimation, and his libertine conversation with me, I fear, does not merit her. Aye! there's the sting; for, were I assured that Maria was happy, my heart is not so selfish but that it would dilate in knowing it, even though it were with another. But to know she is unhappy!—I must drive these thoughts from me. Charlotte has some books; and this is what I believe she calls her little library.

[*Enters a closet.*
Enter DIMPLE *leading* LETITIA.

LETITIA: And will you pretend to say now, Mr. Dimple, that you propose to break with Maria? Are not the banns published? Are not the clothes purchased? Are not the friends invited? In short, is it not a done affair?

DIMPLE: Believe me, my dear Letitia, I would not marry her.

LETITIA: Why have you not broke with her before this, as you all along deluded me by saying you would?

DIMPLE: Because I was in hopes she would, ere this, have broke with me.

LETITIA: You could not expect it.

DIMPLE: Nay, but be calm a moment; 'twas from my regard to you that I did not discard her.

LETITIA: Regard to me!

DIMPLE: Yes; I have done everything in my power to break with her, but the foolish girl is so fond of me that nothing can accomplish it. Besides, how can I offer her my hand when my heart is indissolubly engaged to you?

LETITIA: There may be reason in this; but why so attentive to Miss Manly?

DIMPLE: Attentive to Miss Manly! For heaven's sake, if you have no better opinion of my constancy, pay not so ill a compliment to my taste.

LETITIA: Did I not see you whisper her to-day?

DIMPLE: Possibly I might—but something of so very trifling a nature that I have already forgot what it was.

LETITIA: I believe she has not forgot it.

DIMPLE: My dear creature, how can you for a moment suppose I should have any serious thoughts of that trifling, gay, flighty coquette, that disagreeable—

Enter CHARLOTTE.

DIMPLE: My dear Miss Manly, I rejoice to see you; there is a charm in your conversation that always marks your entrance into company as fortunate.

LETITIA: Where have you been, my dear?

CHARLOTTE: Why, I have been about to twenty shops, turning over pretty things, and so have left twenty visits unpaid. I wish you would step into the carriage and whisk round, make my apology, and leave my cards where our friends are not at home; that, you know, will serve as a visit. Come, do go.

LETITIA: So anxious to get me out! but I'll watch you. [*Aside.*] Oh! yes, I'll go; I want a little exercise. Positively [*Dimple offering to accompany her*], Mr. Dimple, you shall not go; why, half my visits are cake and caudle visits;[48] it won't do, you know, for you to go.

[*Exit, but returns to the door in the back scene and listens.*]

DIMPLE: This attachment of your brother to Maria is fortunate.

CHARLOTTE: How did you come to the knowledge of it?

DIMPLE: I read it in their eyes.

CHARLOTTE: And I had it from her mouth. It would have amused you to have seen her! She, that thought it so great an impropriety to praise a gentleman that she could not bring out one word in your favour, found a redundancy to praise him.

DIMPLE: I have done everything in my power to assist his passion there: your delicacy, my dearest girl, would be shocked at half the instances of neglect and misbehaviour.

Charlotte: I don't know how I should bear neglect; but Mr. Dimple must misbehave himself indeed, to forfeit my good opinion.

DIMPLE: Your good opinion, my angel, is the pride and pleasure of my heart; and if the most respectful tenderness for you, and an utter indifference for all your sex besides, can make me worthy of your esteem, I shall richly merit it.

---

[48] Cake and caudle visits: visits to women who had just given birth or to those who were otherwise indisposed. Caudle is a drink made of warm, sweetened gruel, given chiefly to the sick, women recovering from childbirth, and their visitors.

CHARLOTTE: All my sex besides, Mr. Dimple!—you forgot your tête-à-tête with Letitia.

DIMPLE: How can you, my lovely angel, cast a thought on that insipid, wry-mouthed, ugly creature!

CHARLOTTE: But her fortune may have charms?

DIMPLE: Not to a heart like mine. The man, who has been blessed with the good opinion of my Charlotte, must despise the allurements of fortune.

CHARLOTTE: I am satisfied.

DIMPLE: Let us think no more on the odious subject, but devote the present hour to happiness.

CHARLOTTE: Can I be happy when I see the man I prefer going to be married to another?

DIMPLE: Have I not already satisfied my charming angel, that I can never think of marrying the puling Maria? But, even if it were so, could that be any bar to our happiness? for, as the poet sings,

> "Love, free as air, at sight of human ties,
> Spreads his light wings, and in a moment flies."[49]

Come, then, my charming angel! why delay our bliss? The present moment is ours; the next is in the hand of fate. [*Kissing her.*]

CHARLOTTE: Begone, Sir! By your delusions you had almost lulled my honour asleep.

DIMPLE: Let me lull the demon to sleep again with kisses. [*He struggles with her; she screams.*]

Enter MANLY.

MANLY: Turn, villain! and defend yourself.—[*Draws.*]

[VAN ROUGH *enters and beats down their swords.*]

VAN ROUGH: Is the devil in you? are you going to murder one another? [*Holding Dimple.*]

DIMPLE: Hold him, hold him,—I can command my passion.

---

[49] From Alexander Pope's "Eloisa to Abelard" (1717).

Enter JONATHAN.

JONATHAN: What the rattle ails you? Is the old one[50] in you? Let the colonel alone, can't you? I feel chock-full of fight,—do you want to kill the colonel?—

MANLY: Be still, Jonathan; the gentleman does not want to hurt me.

JONATHAN: Gor! I—I wish he did; I'd shew him Yankee boys play, pretty quick.—Don't you see you have frightened the young woman into the *hystrikes*?[51]

VAN ROUGH: Pray, some of you explain this; what has been the occasion of all this racket?

MANLY: That gentleman can explain it to you; it will be a very diverting story for an intended father-in-law to hear.

VAN ROUGH: How was this matter, Mr. Van Dumpling?

DIMPLE: Sir,—upon my honour,—all I know is, that I was talking to this young lady, and this gentleman broke in on us in a very extraordinary manner.

VAN ROUGH: Why, all this is nothing to the purpose; [*to Charlotte*] can you explain it, Miss?

Enter LETITIA *through the back scene.*

LETITIA: I can explain it to that gentleman's confusion. [*To Van Rough*] Though long betrothed to your daughter, yet, allured by my fortune, it seems (with shame do I speak it) he has privately paid his addresses to me. I was drawn in to listen to him by his assuring me that the match was made by his father without his consent, and that he proposed to break with Maria, whether he married me or not. But, whatever were his intentions respecting your daughter, Sir, even to me he was false; for he has repeated the same story, with some cruel reflections upon my person, to Miss Manly.

JONATHAN: What a tarnal curse!

LETITIA: Nor is this all, Miss Manly. When he was with me this very morning, he made the same ungenerous reflections upon the weakness of your mind as he has so recently done upon the defects of my person.

---

[50] The old one: Satan.

[51] *Hystrikes*: hysterics.

Frontispiece from *The Contrast,* 1790. This illustration depicts the play's
final scene. Van Rough bursts in as Jonathan, who stands at center stage,
challenges a bewigged and ruffled Dimple, warning "I feel chock full of
fight." A uniformed Manly appears to comfort his shaken but lavishly
dressed sister Charlotte. Courtesy of American Antiquarian Society.

JONATHAN: What a tarnal curse and damn, too!

DIMPLE: Ha! since I have lost Letitia, I believe I had as good make it up with Maria. Mr. Van Rough, at present I cannot enter into particulars; but, I believe, I can explain everything to your satisfaction in private.

VAN ROUGH: There is another matter, Mr. Van Dumpling, which I would have you explain. Pray, Sir, have Messrs. Van Cash & Co. presented you those bills for acceptance?

DIMPLE [*aside*]: The deuce! Has he heard of those bills! Nay, then, all's up with Maria, too; but an affair of this sort can never prejudice me among the ladies; they will rather long to know what the dear creature possesses to make him so agreeable. [*To Manly*] Sir, you'll hear from me.

MANLY: And you from me, Sir—

DIMPLE: Sir, you wear a sword—

MANLY: Yes, Sir. This sword was presented to me by that brave Gallic hero, the Marquis De la Fayette.[52] I have drawn it in the service of my country, and in private life, on the only occasion where a man is justified in drawing his sword, in defence of a lady's honour. I have fought too many battles in the service of my country to dread the imputation of cowardice. Death from a man of honour would be a glory you do not merit; you shall live to bear the insult of man and the contempt of that sex whose general smiles afforded you all your happiness.

DIMPLE: You won't meet me, Sir? Then I'll post you for a coward.

MANLY: I'll venture that, Sir. The reputation of my life does not depend upon the breath of a Mr. Dimple. I would have you to know, however, Sir, that I have a cane to chastise the insolence of a scoundrel, and a sword and the good laws of my country to protect me from the attempts of an assassin—

DIMPLE: Mighty well! Very fine, indeed! Ladies and gentlemen, I take my leave; and you will please to observe in the case of my deportment the contrast between a gentleman who has read Chesterfield and received the polish of Europe and an unpolished, untravelled American.

[*Exit.*

---

[52] Marquis de Lafayette (1757–1834) was a young French nobleman who served in the Continental Army. He was a hero in the United States and a close associate of George Washington.

Enter MARIA.

MARIA: Is he indeed gone?—

LETITIA: I hope, never to return.

VAN ROUGH: I am glad I heard of those bills; though it's plaguy unlucky; I hoped to see Mary married before I died.

MANLY: Will you permit a gentleman, Sir, to offer himself as a suitor to your daughter? Though a stranger to you, he is not altogether so to her, or unknown in this city. You may find a son-in-law of more fortune, but you can never meet with one who is richer in love for her, or respect for you.

VAN ROUGH: Why, Mary, you have not let this gentleman make love to you without my leave?

MANLY: I did not say, Sir—

MARIA: Say, Sir!—I—the gentleman, to be sure, met me accidentally.

VAN ROUGH: Ha, ha, ha! Mark me, Mary; young folks think old folks to be fools; but old folks know young folks to be fools. Why, I knew all about this affair. This was only a cunning way I had to bring it about. Hark ye! I was in the closet when you and he were at our house. [*Turns to the company.*] I heard that little baggage say she loved her old father, and would die to make him happy! Oh! how I loved the little baggage! And you talked very prudently, young man. I have inquired into your character, and find you to be a man of punctuality and mind the main chance. And so, as you love Mary and Mary loves you, you shall have my consent immediately to be married. I'll settle my fortune on you, and go and live with you the remainder of my life.

MANLY: Sir, I hope—

VAN ROUGH: Come, come, no fine speeches; mind the main chance, young man, and you and I shall always agree.

LETITIA: I sincerely wish you joy [*advancing to Maria*]; and hope your pardon for my conduct.

MARIA: I thank you for your congratulations, and hope we shall at once forget the wretch who has given us so much disquiet, and the trouble that he has occasioned.

CHARLOTTE: And I, my dear Maria,—how shall I look up to you for forgiveness? I, who, in the practice of the meanest arts, have violated the most sacred rights of friendship? I can never forgive myself, or hope charity from the world; but, I confess, I have much to hope from such a brother; and I am happy that I may soon say, such a sister.

MARIA: My dear, you distress me; you have all my love.

MANLY: And mine.

CHARLOTTE: If repentance can entitle me to forgiveness, I have already much merit; for I despise the littleness of my past conduct. I now find that the heart of any worthy man cannot be gained by invidious attacks upon the rights and characters of others;—by countenancing the addresses of a thousand;—or that the finest assemblage of features, the greatest taste in dress, the genteelest address, or the most brilliant wit, cannot eventually secure a coquette from contempt and ridicule.

MANLY: And I have learned that probity, virtue, honour, though they should not have received the polish of Europe, will secure to an honest American the good graces of his fair countrywomen, and, I hope, the applause of THE PUBLIC.

The End.

3

Primary Documents

A. Arts and Literature in Post-Revolutionary America

Americans debated the place of literature and the arts in the post-revolutionary years, as these two essays from the Columbian Magazine *show. The anonymous author of the first document expressed a common view among post-revolutionary intellectuals, arguing that American republicans could excel in the arts and sciences and that their works should be sources of both amusement and moral instruction. By contrast, the satirical tale of the fictional Augustus Dabbler, the subject of the second document, suggested that not all men of letters were genuinely learned or public-spirited. Indeed, the reader is led to value the spinning and weaving of the rustic Mrs. Dabbler far more than the literary contributions of her self-promoting husband.*

1. THE FORMER, PRESENT, AND FUTURE PROSPECTS OF AMERICA (1786)

The situation of our country is peculiarly happy and agreeable—the purity and serenity of our atmosphere, the moderation of the seasons, all lend an assisting hand to the exertions of the industrious and diligent . . . Nature has been profuse in her blessings. May the omnipotent be as propitious! May he kindly protect us from every misfortune—from venality and vice—effeminacy and luxury—those precursors of political destruction. Thus shall our happiness be as unbounded as creation, and as durable as time.[1]

Circumstanced as we at present are, it would be unpardonable, and it is impossible, but that we should daily increase and improve in arts, manufactures, and literature . . . Countries, and especially republics, in our present circumstances, have been birth-places of eloquence, philosophy, and all the sciences. It was not Athens enslaved and conquered, but still free and triumphant, that reared a Demosthenes to defeat Philip by the thunder of his eloquence, and save the endangered state. It was not Rome, inebriated by luxury, and oppressed by Caesar, that exhibited the genius of freedom in Cicero; who, by the irresistible force of his oratory, preserved the expiring flame of liberty. . . .

Since, then, there is such a natural connection between freedom and eloquence, and since we have been fortunate enough to preserve and secure the former, it becomes us to seek the latter with an unabating ardour. But, for this purpose, other branches of literature, nay, all the arts and sciences, are to be advanced and cultivated. And thus, by a wise intermixture of the *utile* and *dulce,* we shall acquire a greater perfection in each part, and unite pleasure and improvement in the same happy path. Imagination shall assist, cheer, and exhilarate the more solid judgment and reason; while the delightful study of poetry, and eloquence, shall "intersperse with verdure and flowers, the dusky deserts of barren philosophy."

2. THE DABBLERS (1788)

I have been known, Sir, in this city, these nine years, by the name of young Master Dabbler, in distinction from my father, who teaches school at the other end of town. My excellence, however, in politics, poetry, and other of the fine arts, hath kept my attention much of my time from the dull drudgery of my school . . . I have written . . . plays, religious and political controversy, &c. . . . [The local printer] proposes to print them cheap, and wait their sale for his pay; but by various excuses he delays the performance, and has lately used me very ill, by publishing a severe and illiberal reply to one of my songs, calling in question my sense, learning, and principles of honour; all which I hold dearer than life. My spouse, bred in the country, is not a little pleased with this, and flatters herself, that it would discourage me from giving so much of my time to public affairs; but, Mr. Editor, what would become of America, if no one should mind public matters, and what liberties would rulers not take, if persons of genius, did not by their publications, keep them in awe?[2]

Mrs. Dabbler frequently receives flax and wool from her father in the country, and I am not a little hindered in my studies, by the noise of her wheel, for which to no purpose, I often check her. She has, indeed, kept our two children by this means in comfortable apparel, and kept me from the cold. But we can appear in no style in this home-made dress, now worn by none of taste, and as I have often told her, if once I could get my works printed, and a few thousand sold, we might shew our importance.

My father-in-law, a plain farmer, is always advising me in his own silly, rustic way, to quit the city, and live with him, and has offered me half of his small farm, on condition that I will live on it, and work it myself. To which I have at length agreed, and a conveyance of it on those conditions is to be made next Monday, by Mr. Sly, a neighbouring attorney; who, by the by, understands his business, is a very clever man, and my friend; and says, if I can advance him a guinea, he will insert some learned, ambiguous, and evasive terms of law, that will enable me to sell the land to any one, and use the money as I please.

Now, Mr. Editor, what I would propose to you, is this: you have seen how great use I am to our printer, and why may I not serve you in the same way? Your works, in prose or verse, would then make a respectable figure, . . . never wanting interesting and elegant matter, especially for or against the new constitution; and though I never went through the college, I have *Cole's dictionary*, which will help me now and then to a Latin term, or motto. . . .

DISCUSSION QUESTIONS

1. How did each author envision the relationship between the arts and republican ideals? How did each see the role of artists and writers in post-revolutionary America?

2. How do you think readers of the *Columbian Magazine* reacted to the character of Augustus Dabbler, and to that of Mrs. Dabbler? What lessons were readers supposed to learn from the Dabblers' tale?

3. These two pieces appeared in the same publication, the *Columbian Magazine,* within two years of each other. Do you think that the editors of the *Columbian Magazine* modified their views about the place of literature and writers in American society?

B. Virtues and Vices of the Theater

Outlawed in many colonies and included among the luxuries proscribed by the Continental Association in 1774, professional theater remained controversial in post-revolutionary America. Defenders of the theater, like those citizens who unsuccessfully sought its legalization in Massachusetts in 1792, argued that polite and wholesome plays could enhance the manners and morals of those who viewed them. The first document contains excerpts from an anonymous pamphlet by Boston theater proponent William Haliburton, who illustrates this view. The theater's critics used an array of religious, moral, and economic arguments to condemn the stage and its allegedly ruinous effects on popular behavior and values. The second document, below, is a petition that "sundry citizens" addressed to the Pennsylvania state legislature as part of an unsuccessful attempt to oppose the opening of theaters in post-revolutionary Philadelphia.

1. EFFECTS OF THE STAGE ON THE MANNERS OF A PEOPLE (1792)

A man while a living actor on the stage of the world, becometh both precept and example to others; the view and consideration of his virtues will effectuate more than volumes of sermons; his crimes, his follies and his fate become in the mouth of wisdom, lectures on prudence and the most forcible admonitions to her attentive pupils. His conduct is recorded in the volume of history, whose page is appointed to blazon his prudence or his folly for the instruction of succeeding generations.[3]

There are, comparatively speaking, but few who of those who read history, that can enter into its true spirit, or derive to themselves any advantage from it . . . Hence the Stage would become to America . . . the nurse of wisdom . . . All farces, pantomimes, low-jesting, witticisms, buffoonery, rope-dancing, &c. (which serve only to waste the time and money of the people without any one benefit in return; and have moreover an evident tendency to deprave their taste and corrupt their morals) should be forever banished [from] the Theatre, and all places of public resort, as infinitely beneath the dignity of a polite and sensible people. . . .

As a created, dependant being, and as a member of society, man hath several relative offices and duties. With respect to his intercourse with the Deity, each one hath right to think and act for himself; but whatever relates to society, and the due ordering thereof, generally or particularly becomes an object of government . . . Knowledge, industry, economy, cleanliness, temperance, sobriety, sincerity, justice, benevolence, the love or order, and love of country, are all of infinite concern to the state, to society, and to individuals; and therefore of the highest political importance to government . . . And as the Stage hath the most immediate, intimate and affecting relation to the several advantages and virtues here mentioned, the *erecting* and *correcting* of the stage, the support, encouragement, and continuance thereof, becomes directly . . . a most important concern of government. . . .

There are two ways of reforming mankind, politically and morally; the effects of the Stage are great in both! . . . The stage is properly connected with government, an engine in their hands, to *impel, direct*, or *restrain* the spirits of a nation! It becomes part of the administration of the *public* weal; reforms as much of the morals, as relates to society, the rest it leaves to heaven! . . .

Government will do well to consider the state of society in Boston and the other towns under their care; they cannot but observe, that the people are left much to their own heads; that the *fervour* of religion is much abated, that interested and selfish designs begin to triumph over morality, and are daily gaining ground . . . That those persons who attend many hours to study, business, or labour, want something to unbend and amuse their minds . . . many there are, who, after the fatigues of the day, resort to gaming-houses, taverns, &c. and when heated with liquor, resort to still worse places; the consequences whereof may be better imagined than recounted. . . .

Would it not be proper, honourable, and becoming the dignity of a free, enlightened government, to consider more attentively, the greater and lesser divisions on the scale of equal liberty? . . . Will it be betraying the trust reposed in them, or departing from their dignity, to consider, that the sensible, polite inhabitants of Boston (many of them) are desirous and anxious to have a Theatre, where they may pass the hours of relaxation, after the fatigues of the day; where they may hope to be amused and instructed without injury, prejudice, or inconvenience to any; and without offending against the law?

Those of the subjects who oppose it, ought to consider, whether they have any right to prevent others from enjoying such amusements as they are fond of? . . . Can such opposition be justified on any principles whatsoever?

In a country where clime, soil, and aliments, (operating on the clear perceptions of native genius) promise as much for the Americans as any people now in being; with a rising character among the nations what can, or will, expand their powers, or mature and perfect their genius, like a well regulated Theatre, supported by the most affecting and animating music?

It was neither the clime, genius, nor constitutions of Greece and Rome, that alone raised them to that distinction and celebrity in the annals of mankind: It was their Theatres and music, together with their games, which inspired, improved and elevated them. Such, and even greater (the extent, numbers, and commerce of the Union, considered) may be their effects in America. . . .

2. ANTI-THEATER PETITION (1793)

That being certainly informed that a Petition is now preferred to this Honourable House, for repealing the law for the suppression of vice and immorality, as far as it relates to the acting of plays in this state . . . we flatter ourselves you will bear with us while we give our reasons for this Remonstrance.[4]

First. The diversion of the stage is contrary to the Holy Scripture. There is reason to believe the Apostle Paul intended a prohibition of this, when he says, *"Neither filthiness nor foolish talking and jesting, which are not convenient."* It is true the word plays is not mentioned in Scripture, neither do we read of a prohibition in so many words against "masquerades, routs, &c." yet none will pretend a warrant for them from the sacred oracles.

Second. Let plays be never so well regulated they are inconsistent with the Christian character. The design of the Christian religion is to moderate our passions and appetites, and keep them within proper bounds. All recreations that are of an intoxicating nature should be avoided; of this sort we apprehend are plays . . . Much is said in praise of tragedies communicating useful instruction to mankind. But as there are so many bad characters represented as has a tendency to familiarize sin to those who see it committed. It is inconsistent with the Christian character to witness the bad actions of men, even where they are only exhibited by representation.

Third. The first intention of plays is amusement . . . Now the great design of amusement is for those who stand in need of relaxation, either by bodily labour or hard study: of those who are the attendants of plays few come within this description. But admitting they did, the theatre is unsuitable as an amusement because it consumes too much time, and is carried to that hour of the night which is proper for sleep: it agitates the passions too much for an amusement, which exhausts instead of invigorating and relaxing the spirits. The exhibition of imaginary distress seldom fails to produce real [agitation] in the minds of the spectators. Besides, it is an amusement that is very expensive, while other ways which answer the purpose better, may be easily attained. The rich may feel no force in this, but the rage for pleasure pushes many to throw that money away for plays that should support their families and pay their just debts.

Fourth. Attending plays, and that by public authority, is encouraging players in their unchristian profession. Their profession is to amuse their fellow-creatures, and this is a shocking prostitution of the rational powers to give amusement to the idle part of mankind. What a strange character, to live perpetually in a mask? To be much oftener in a personated than a real character? What polluted minds must those have who are a receptacle of foreign vanities, where one system or plan of folly is only obliterated to make way for another? The business of the play actor is to express the language and exhibit a perfect picture of the character of vicious men. He must enter into the spirit and feel the sentiments proper to their character. Hence it often happens, that their characters are a living copy of that vanity, obscenity, and impiety, which is to be found in the pieces which they represent. And shall the professors of the holy religion of Jesus Christ support men in such a character? and shall their profession have the sanction of law?

Fifth. Plays are peculiarly dangerous to youth. Attending plays make them vie with each other in luxury of dress. Their minds acquire insensibly an inclination to romance and extravagance, and thereby become unfitted for the sober and serious affairs of common life. They are apt to despise ordinary business as mean, or deride it as ridiculous. Will the merchant chuse that his apprentice learn exactness and frugality from the stage? Do those whose generosity is strengthened by weeping over virtue in distress, make the most punctual payments? To a tradesman's wife or daughter, how mean and contemptible do the affairs of their family appear, after seeing the gaudy scenes of the stage, and how apt are they to be afterwards misguided or neglected? The actors themselves are a proof of this . . . To learn morality from them is to learn piety from the profane, mortification from the sensual, and modesty from an harlot.

Sixth. To open the theatre which we shut in the time of public calamity, as a public evil, and then reckoned a vice, is very ungrateful to the Lord our God, who has so wonderfully interposed in our behalf, and crowned the war with Liberty, Peace, and Independence. His goodness should lead us to repentance, upon meeting with such signal mercies. We ought devoutly to pray to the Lord *"That he would grant unto us, that we being delivered out of the hand of our enemies, might serve him without fear, in holiness and righteousness before him all the days of our life."* It is laid down as a maxim, that a republican form of government cannot exist without Virtue in the people; we therefore consider every thing that tends to promote the cause of immorality, as a stroke at our civil Liberty. *"Righteousness exalteth a nation, but sin is the reproach of any people."*

DISCUSSION QUESTIONS

1. What sorts of people were likely to oppose the theater? What sorts were likely to support it?
2. How did the pro- and anti-theater authors think about leisure? What did each group see as the purpose of amusements for post-revolutionary Americans?
3. Why did many post-revolutionary Americans believe that government could—and even should—regulate public amusements? Can you think of any modern debates that resemble the battle over the stage in post-revolutionary America?

C. *Lord Chesterfield and His Critics*

First published in America in 1775, Lord Chesterfield's Letters of Advice to His Son *remained popular in the United States well into the nineteenth century. Chesterfield's letters taught generations of readers the "art of pleasing," which he considered the key to worldly success. The letters of this English aristocrat, which stressed outward demeanor over inner character, appealed to ambitious readers of all social ranks in post-revolutionary America. But Chesterfield also had many critics, in both Europe and the United States. For example, the renown American playwright and historian, Mercy Otis Warren, whose letter to her own son appears below, decried the moral implications of Chesterfield's praise for pretense and also his lack of respect for women. Penned as part of a private letter in 1779, Warren's criticisms of Chesterfield appeared in print in three different Boston periodicals (the* Independent Chronicle, Boston Magazine, *and* Massachusetts Magazine*) in 1781, 1784, and 1790, respectively.*

1. THE ART OF PLEASING MEN AND WOMEN (1747)

Dear Boy:

The art of pleasing is a very necessary one to possess; but a very difficult one to acquire. It can hardly be reduced to rules; and your own good sense and observation will teach you more of it than I can. 'Do as you would be done by,' is the surest method that I know of pleasing. Observe carefully what pleases you in others, and probably the same thing in you will please others. If you are pleased with the complaisance and attention of others to your humours, your tastes, or your weaknesses, depend upon it, the same complaisance and attention on your part, to theirs, will equally please them. Take the tone of the company that you are in, and do not pretend to give it; be serious, gay, or even trifling, as you find the present humour of the company; this is an attention due from every individual to the majority. . . .[5]

If you would particularly gain the affection and friendship of particular people, whether men or women, endeavour to find out the predominant excellency, if they have one, and their prevailing weakness, which everybody has; and do justice to the one, and something more than justice to the other. Men have various objects in which they may excel, or at least would be thought to excel; and, though they love to hear justice done to them, where they know that they excel, yet they are most and best flattered upon those points where they wish to excel, and yet are doubtful whether they do or not . . . You will easily discover every man's prevailing vanity, by observing his favourite topic of conversation; for every man talks most of what he has most a mind to be thought to excel in. Touch him but there, and you touch him to the quick. . . .

Women have, in general, but one object, which is their beauty; upon which, scarce any flattery is too gross for them to follow. Nature has hardly formed a woman ugly enough to be insensible to flattery upon her person; if her face is so shocking that she must, in some degree, be conscious of it, her figure and her air, she trusts, make ample amends for it. If her figure is deformed, her face, she thinks, counterbalances it. If they are both bad, she comforts herself that she has graces . . . still more engaging than beauty.

This truth is evident, from the studied and elaborate dress of the ugliest women in the world. An undoubted, uncontested, conscious beauty, is of all women, the least sensible of flattery upon that head; she knows that it is her due, and is therefore obliged to nobody for giving it her. She must be flattered upon her understanding; which, though she may possibly not doubt of herself, yet she suspects that men may distrust.

2. Mercy Otis Warren on Chesterfield's Letters (1779)

My Dear Son,

I perceive, by your last, you are enraptured with Lord Chesterfield, nor do I wonder at it. I should have no opinion of your taste if you was not charmed with the correct style, the elegant diction, the harmony of language, the thousand beauties of expression, that run parallel with the knowledge of the world and the arts of life, through this complete system of refinement. This masterly writer has furnished the present generation with a code of politeness which perhaps surpasses any thing of the kind in the English language. But when he sacrifices truth to convenience, probity to pleasure, virtue to the graces, generosity, gratitude, and all the fine feelings of the soul, to a momentary gratification, we cannot but pity the man as much as we admire the author: And I never see this fascinating collection of letters taken up by the youthful reader, but I

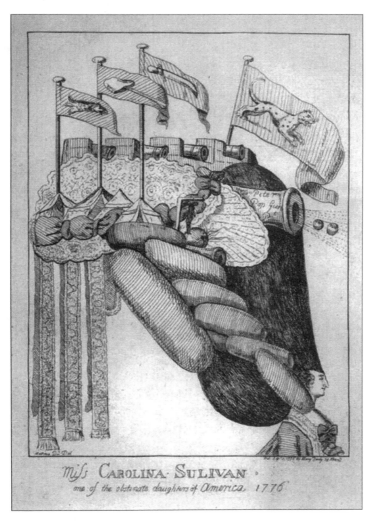

Miss Carolina Sullivan, one of the obstinate daughters of America, 1776

Miss Carolina Sullivan, 1776. Although men were clearly susceptible to the allure of fashion, contemporaries (including Chesterfield and the anonymous creator of this English cartoon) were far more likely to satirize women for their vanity and fashion consciousness. This image mocks the elaborate hairstyles of elite women by linking them to the colonial defense of Charleston, South Carolina, in 1776. The artist suggests that colonial military efforts, like these female hairstyles, were foolish and artificial. Among patriotic Americans, the cartoon reinforced the perception that English fashions were politically suspect. Library of Congress.

tremble, lest the honeyed poison that lurks beneath the fairest flowers of fancy and rhetorick, should leave a deeper tincture on the mind, than even his documents for external decency and the semblance of morality. I have no quarrel with the *Graces* . . . and all the innocent arts of engaging the esteem and alluring the affections of mankind. The passion is laudable, and may be indulged to the highest pitch consistent with the eternal law of rectitude. But I love better that frankness and sincerity that bespeaks a soul above dissimulation; that genuine, resolute, manly fortitude, that equally despises and resists the temptation to vice, in the purlieus of the brothel, or the antechamber of the princess; in the arms of the emaciated, distempered prostitute, or beneath the smile of the painted courtesan, who decorates her guilty charms even with the blandishments of honour. And however ennobled by birth, dignified by rank, or justly admired for his literary productions, I must beg leave to differ from his Lordship, and think it by no means necessary, that a gentleman, in order to be initiated into the science of good breeding, should drop his humanity; that to acquire a courtly mien, and become an adept in politeness, he should renounce the moral feelings; or to be master of the graces, that his life should be a contrast to every principle of christianity.[6]

Can there be a portrait more unnatural or deformed, or an object more completely ridiculous, than that of a father exerting all the powers of brilliant talents, aided by the chicanery of subtle politicians, the false reasoning of the infidel tribe, and the vulgar witticisms from Julius Caesar to Borgia, to arouse the corrupt passions in the bosom of his son, to inflame the desires, and to urge those loose gratifications, which it has been the work of ages to counteract, by all the arguments of reason, religion and philosophy . . . ?

His Lordship's severity to the ladies, . . . his trite, vulgar, hackneyed observations, the contempt he affects to pour on so fair a part of the creation, are as much beneath the resentment of a woman of education and reflection, as they are derogatory to the candour and generosity of a writer of his acknowledged abilities and fame.

I believe in this age of refinement and philosophy, few men indulge a peculiar asperity with regard to the sex in general, but such as have been unfortunate in their acquaintance, unsuccessful in their address, or soured from repeated disappointments. And however practicable this connoisseur in the spirit of intrigue, might announce the conquest of the whole sex, it has been asserted by one of his biographers, that he was never known to be successful in any of his gallantries, but that which brought Mr. Stanhope [Chesterfield's illegitimate son] into the world.

I have ever considered human nature as the same in both sexes; nor perhaps is the soul very differently modified by the vehicle in which it is placed. The foibles, the passions, the vices and the virtues, appear to spring from the same source; and, under similar advantages, frequently reach the same degree of perfection, or sink to the same stages of depravity, which so often stamp disgrace on the human form. Yet custom, in most countries, has branded licentious manners, in female life, with peculiar marks of infamy; but we live in days happily adroit in the arts of removing every impediment to pleasure, when the bars of rectitude are systematically reasoned down, and no other distinction is necessary but a dextrous talent at concealment.

It may perhaps be deemed presumptuous for a woman to speak thus freely of so celebrated a work as [Chesterfield's] Advice; but I shall yet venture to say more, as I have read his letters with attention, much more with a view to the happiness of some I love, than for my own pleasure or advantage; and I think them crowded with a repetition of the most trifling injunctions, replete with observations, rules and precepts, exceedingly advantageous for the conduct of younger life; but marked with the most atrocious license of thought, and stained with insinuations subversive of every moral and religious principle.

DISCUSSION QUESTIONS

1. In *The Contrast*, both Billy Dimple and his servant, Jessamy, profess to be disciples of Chesterfield. How do the different social ranks of these characters influence the ways in which they interpret and act on Chesterfield's advice?
2. What did Mercy Otis Warren find appealing in Chesterfield's letters? What did she find objectionable?
3. Compare and contrast Chesterfield's and Warren's views of human nature. How did each understand the differences between the sexes and relationships between men and women?

D. The Follies of Fashion

In April 1787, advertisements for The Contrast *appeared in the same issues of the* New York *Daily Advertiser which carried the following two essays. The anonymous author, who adopted the pseudonym "A Republican," criticized the extravagant styles of clothing favored by the city's women and men on political, economic, and moral grounds. Like Royall Tyler, this essayist saw clothing and fashion as cultural markers. However, while* The Contrast *conveyed Tyler's somewhat ambivalent stance on the subjects of fashion and dress, "A Republican" used language reminiscent of colonial patriots to condemn English-style luxury and extravagance. Equating the renunciation of English fashions with opposition to tyranny, the essayist connected stylish clothing with selfishness and anti-republican political values.*

1. FOR THE FEMALES (1787)

Ladies attend; pray hear what a plain honest Republican has to say; and if you think as he does, you will immediately alter the present fashions, and introduce frugality, economy, and industry, the pillars which support a democratic government.[7]

Since we have no more connection with Great-Britain, is it not highly ridiculous to follow them in all the extravagancies which they have introduced, especially as a spirit of luxury and dissipation must inevitably overthrow the fair Temple of Liberty, which has been reared by the blood of our bravest heroes.

These things perhaps will be looked upon by some females, as idle and ridiculous nonsense; but the patriotic fair (and some of this class I trust there are still) will raise their thoughts beyond the trifling ornaments of dress, and prize the welfare of their country before those foreign gew-gaws which ill become a Republican.

Consider for a moment what an amazing tax we pay to England for gauzes, ribbons, silks, laces, and a thousand other trifles, made at a small expence, and transported three thousand miles, to gratify the fancies of Americans! Surely this is folly and imprudence. . . .

Fashions are generally introduced by the higher class, from them they descend down to the lower rank. For instance, if lady _____ gets a new hat or dress from England, Miss must buy one also, then her acquain-

The Toilet, 1786. This English mezzotint by an unknown artist
suggests that fashionably fastidious women arouse the passions and
cloud the judgment of otherwise reasonable men. Its caption reads:
With winning coyness she my Soul disarms, / Her face darts forth a
thousand rays, / My eyeballs Swim, & I grow giddy while I gaze.
Courtesy of the Lewis Walpole Library, Yale University.

tance cannot be so vulgar, but she must have the same . . . Thus the females copy after one and another, and if a lady of *taste* wears a new cap
or gown at church you may be sure the next Sunday to see half the con-
gregation sporting the fashion. I hope, however, they will attend to
these things, and by discouraging that spirit of dissipation and extravagance which prevails so much at present, set an example of economy

that will convince the world they are emulous to advance the glory and happiness of the American continent.

The fair of this city are particularly called upon to bring about a reformation in their dress. Throw aside your large hoops, burn your bishops, and pull down those *false bosoms* which appear to every modest person as objects of temptation for the gentlemen. In short, be more decent in the manufactures, and despise every fashion that would tend to make you appear more like dissipated depraved Europeans, than plain, simple Americans.

2. FANTASTICAL, PREPOSTEROUS FASHIONS [OF] GENTLEMEN (1787)

When an apprentice . . . leaves London and comes over to this country, he immediately sets up for a beau or fine gentleman; powders [his hair], dresses in the tip of the mode, with his round shoe buckles, high caped coat, and octagon buttons, ruffle shirt and silk stockings; by using a few polite phrases and assuming an air of consequence, endeavours to ingratiate himself into the opinion of our ladies for a *monstrous pretty fellow*.[8]

If he honors the theatre with his company, you may be sure to see him stuck up in a front box, with his back turned towards the stage; damning the actors for a parcel of stupid performers; thinks the audience *vastly vulgar* and *ungenteel,* and would faint away were he not relieved by a smelling bottle. . . .

Thus do the young Englishmen shew their good breeding when they come to this country, and set an example which I am sorry to say is too much followed by numbers of our American youth. When such upstarts as I have just described arrive here, they are noticed by the females, and receive as much attention from the fair, as is possible for them to bestow on the truly polite man.

Is it not surprising then that the ladies complain of the ungallantry of their own citizens, when they countenance every London shop-boy who is so fortunate as to get clear of the counter and puts on their airs of a person of quality?

Surely an American must be divested of common sensibility that can visit and pay attention to those females who prefer the company of a sinical foreigner before that of the natives.

A Morning Ramble, or, The Milliner's Shop, 1782. Fashion-starved Americans resumed shopping with a vengeance after the war was over. This unsigned English mezzotint portrays the milliner's shop as the site of flirtation, luxury—even the dog is coiffed!—and artifice. Boxes on the shelves bear the labels "feathers," "love," "coxcomb," and "mode." While one gentleman leers at the working milliner, another hands out tickets to a masquerade. Courtesy of the Lewis Walpole Library, Yale University.

If our young men were to devote that time which is taken up in dress, to the study of our constitution, the principles of a republican government, and the many other branches of knowledge which every free American should be acquainted with, we should see our youth springing up, prepared to serve their country in the cabinet or field. Such conduct far better becomes republicans, than that spirit of dissipation and fondness for dress which at present so universally prevails.

Let men clothe themselves in the manufactures of our own productions, study the profession of a soldier before that of a beau; discourage every article of dress which would effeminate the man and corrupt the morals; despise all these forward impertinent persons who assume the character of gentlemen, and by treating them with that contempt their insignificancy deserves, force them to follow those fashions which should be plain, neat and simple.

DISCUSSION QUESTIONS

1. Why did "A Republican" see current fashions in clothing as dangerous to Americans?
2. Which, if any, of his observations about New Yorkers in 1787 are evident in Royall Tyler's characters? Based on your reading of *The Contrast,* do you think that Tyler agreed with the essayist's assessment of the relative roles of men and women in the promotion of fashion?
3. How and why, according to "A Republican," did fashions spread among women and men? Did the behavior of the characters in *The Contrast* support the essayist's view?

E. The Ideal Wife

Most eighteenth-century people considered marriage the ideal state for women and men. They also believed that family life, in general, brought both personal and public benefits. After the Revolution, however, Americans entered into an unprecedented debate on the appropriate roles of husbands and wives. On the one hand, custom and the English common law deemed wives weak, dependent, and subordinate. On the other, newer ideas about feminine virtue and sensibility, along with women's patriotism in the recent war, led many to advocate more equal relations between the sexes. The documents below, an essay by "A Matrimonial Republican," which appeared in the Lady's Magazine, *and an excerpt from a conduct manual for women written by Dr. Samuel K. Jennings, a male physician, represent versions of each of these views.*

1. ON MATRIMONIAL OBEDIENCE (1792)

I object to the word *obey* in the marriage-service, (and I dare say many ladies have objected to it on the same account) because it is a general word, without limitation or definition. My dictionary tells me what it is *to obey* and the word in our marriage-service, admits of no exceptions: it is *obey* in its fullest sense. The bride, who should pronounce the word *obey* with mental reservations, would certainly deceive herself, if she supposed she would not be guilty of a species of perjury; for where I have sworn, or even promised to obey any man, I must on honour consider myself as having sworn or promised to obey him, in all things, and at all times. In a word, I have bound myself to be his slave, until he is pleased to release me, which in the matrimonial world, is an occurrence that I believe seldom happens. And in doing this, I think it will not be denied that I am a slave to all intents and purposes; intents in which I have no design, and purposes in which I have no interest, and from which I derive no happiness.[9]

But we are not accustomed in this liberal age to consider the marriage engagement as a contract of this kind. Why, therefore, is the word *obey* still preserved in our service, when it would be so easy to leave it out; and when, in fact we know that it is virtually left out by nine out of ten who enter into that holy state? . . .

In [the cases of children and servants], it is understood that obedience is expected, but that obedience is at the same time understood with proper limitation, otherwise we were a nation of slaves and not freemen. Why then, should the partner of our cares and our sorrows, why should our *wives* only be bound by a promise in which no limitations are expressed? If those limitations are understood, then there is no longer occasion for the word *obey*. . . .

The obedience between man and wife, I conceive, is, or ought to be mutual. It ought to be mutual for the sake of their interest, inasmuch as two free opinions conjoined are much more likely to produce a wise decision, than one haughty and exclusive. And it ought to be mutual for the sake of their happiness; for I believe it will be acknowledged, with conviction on all hands, that whatever miseries arise in the married state, arise from the assumption on one side or other of absolute power. Marriage ought never to be considered as a contract between a superior and an inferior, but a reciprocal union of interest, an implied partnership of interests, where all differences are accommodated by conference;

and where the decision admits of no retrospect. Separate privileges there may be on both sides; but, like the houses of lords and commons, tenacious as they are of their privileges, they should in all disputed points, meet each other half way, and like those houses too, when a question of privilege occurs, always clear the galleries, that there may be no witnesses of the dispute.

If the husband amicably agrees to obey the wife, and the wife to obey the husband, it may perhaps be said, there can be nothing at all done, or that this is absurd in terms; for where there is no command there can be no obedience. Absurd however, as this may appear in theory, it is perfectly reconcilable, and daily practiced in some of the happiest, nay, in all the happy families in this place. A thousand little instances will arise, wherein obedience may be manifested from the husband to the wife, and from the wife to the husband, found too on the best of all possible foundations of obedience, in gratitude; for what is mutual obedience but the gratitude of each party reciprocally for former instances of obedience.

2. Proper Conduct of the Wife Towards Her Husband (1804)

1. As it is your great wish and interest to enjoy much of your husband's company and conversation, it will be important to acquaint yourself with his temper, his inclination, and his manner, that you may render your house, your person and your disposition quite agreeable to him. By observing with accuracy, and guarding your words and actions with prudence, you may quickly succeed according to your wishes.[10]

2. Here perhaps you ask, why so much pains necessary on my part? I will answer your question candidly. Your choice in forming the connexion, was at best a passive one. Could you have acted the part of a courtier and made choice of a man whose disposition might have corresponded precisely with yours, there would have been less to do afterwards. But under present circumstances, it is your interest to adapt yourself to your husband, whatever may be his peculiarities. Again, nature has made man the stronger, the consent of mankind has given him superiority over his wife, his inclination is, to claim his natural and acquired rights. He of course expects from you a degree of condescension, and he feels himself the more confident of the propriety of his claim,

when he is informed, that St. Paul adds his authority to its support. "Wives, submit yourselves unto your own husbands, as unto the Lord, for the husband is the head of his wife."

3. In obedience then to this precept of the gospel, to the laws of custom and nature, you ought to cultivate a cheerful and happy submission. . . .

4. The great affection and submission practised by most men in time of courtship, are well calculated to raise in the female mind, false expectation of an uniform continuance of the same officiousness after marriage. For the honey moon you may not be disappointed. But the charge of a family will soon teach any man, that he has something more to do than live a life of courtship. The discharge of his duty as a father, a friend, and a citizen, will gradually divert him in some degree from that punctilious attention to your person, with which you are so highly pleased.

5. Should you begin to discover this change, be careful to conduct yourself with discretion. By no means upbraid him, nor suffer jealousy to take possession of your breast. If you once admit this passion, it may terminate in your ruin. It will lead you to consider every seeming inattention, as a proof of his want of affection . . . Jealousy once admitted contaminates the soul. . . .

6. As you regard your own bliss, speedily check all thoughts of this kind, as soon as they arise in your mind. If indulged, they will have a baneful effect upon your temper, and spread a gloom over your countenance, so as to strip you of every charm. Your husband repelled from time to time, will at length become indifferent, and leaving you to languish in your distress, he will seek for amusement where it may be found. And thus you will bring upon yourself the very evil, against which you would make your mistaken defence.

7. If you have already proved the truth of these reflections by sad experience, I know you are ready to excuse yourself, because the whole proceeded from the most sincere affection. But you should consider that the anxiety and distress which are so often depicted in your countenance, might with equal propriety, lead your companion to doubt the sincerity of your love. And for any thing you know to the contrary, a suspicion of this kind is at the bottom of the whole mischief. Do not act like stubborn children, rejecting that happiness which is entirely in your own power.

8. If he do not come in, the very hour or day that you expect him,

instead of accusing him with neglect, be the considerate woman, and take into view the various and unavoidable delays with which he must meet in transacting his business. And be assured, for I speak from experience, that in many instances he sacrifices his most sincere wishes to be with you, for what he considers necessary for the present. He is bound to provide for you and your children. In easy circumstances there is most satisfaction, and he feels a strong desire to secure this foundation for your future happiness. Receive him then with gladness as often as he comes in, shew him that you are happy in his company, and let the preparations made for his reception, prove to him, that he holds a considerable share in your thoughts and affections when he is absent. Such conduct will endear you to his heart, and secure to you all the attention and regard you so ardently desire.

9. Do not suppose, that my plan implies that the husband has nothing to do. So far from this he is bound "To love and cherish his wife, as his own flesh." But I repeat it, this obligation seems in a great degree, to rest on the condition of a loving and cheerful submission on the part of the wife. Here again perhaps you object and say, "Why not the husband, first shew a little condescension as well as the wife?" I answer for these plain reasons. It is not his disposition; it is not the custom but with the hen-pecked; it is not his duty; it is not implied in the marriage contract; it is not required by law or gospel.

10. I presume you are not one of those ladies who indulge a mean opinion of their companions, and are indeed ashamed of them. This can happen in no case where there is not a want of information and judgment. If you stooped in marrying him, do not indulge the thought, that you added to his respectability. Never tell him you "lifted him out of the ashes." For it will be hard for you to extricate yourself from this difficulty. If you stooped of necessity, because you could get no one else, the obligation is on your own side. If you stooped of choice, who ought to be blamed but yourself? Besides it will be well to remember that when you became his wife, he became your head, and your supposed superiority was buried in that voluntary act.

DISCUSSION QUESTIONS

1. Why did "A Matrimonial Republican" object to the continued use of the word "obey" in a woman's marriage vows? Do you think that this au-

thor believed that women and men were equal? What was the significance of the author's comparison between the status of women and that
of slaves, servants, and children?

2. What, according to Dr. Samuel K. Jennings, the author of the second document, were the practical and ideological bases of sexual inequality? Is it
significant that Jennings first published his advice to wives in 1804, twelve
years after the publication of the essay by "A Matrimonial Republican"?

3. How did each of these authors envision the ideal marriage and the roles
and responsibilities of married women? What sorts of women were more
likely to identify with the ideals of "A Matrimonial Republican"? What
sorts of women might have found Jennings's advice more relevant or
helpful?

F. The Ideal Husband

*Post-revolutionary debates on the proper roles and demeanor of wives
necessitated reassessment of men's roles and responsibilities as husbands
and fathers. Social critics who argued in favor of companionate marriage also articulated a new masculine ideal, as shown in the first document, an essay from the genteel* Columbian Magazine. *Men's enjoyment
of sensibility and virtue in the domestic sphere, the anonymous author
suggested, would engender public conduct that would benefit the commonwealth. In America as in Europe, such relatively enlightened ideas
coexisted with more traditional notions of patriarchy and misogyny, as
the second essay, from the same publication, shows.*

1. PANEGYRIC ON THE MARRIAGE STATE (1786)

What object, in all nature, can be so beautiful, as that of two young
persons, of amiable lives and tempers, uniting before the altar in vows
of mutual constancy and love—and afterwards proceeding through all
the vicissitudes and accidents of lives, assuaging every evil, and increasing every good, by the most unaffected tenderness? . . .[11]

How tranquil is the state of that bosom which has, as it were, a door
perpetually open to the reception of joy, or departure of pain, by unin-
terrupted confidence in, and sympathy with, the object of its affection!

I know of no part of the single or bachelor's estate, more irksome than the privation we feel by it, of any friendly breast in which to pour our delights, or from whence to extract an antidote for whatever may chance to give us pain. . . . The charms, then, of social life, and the sweets of domestic conversation, are no small incitements to the marriage state. What more agreeable than the conversation of an intelligent, amiable, and interesting friend? But who more intelligent than a well-educated female? What more amiable than gentleness and sensibility itself? Or what friend more interesting than such a one as we have selected from the whole world to be our steady companion, and in every vicissitude of seasons or of life? . . .

Let the lady find agreeable employment at home, in the domestic economy of her household—but let the gentleman be pursuing, by unremitted and honesty industry, new comforts for her—for his children —and for himself. Let, too, the commonwealth have a place in his thoughts; it surely will, in his occupations, if they be of any meritorious kind—for these will ornament his country, whose glory, whose prosperity and fame, he should ever consider essential to his own; remembering, that on these *it* depends; and that this is the smallest tribute he can pay, for the comforts he enjoys, from its soil, its protection, and its laws.

2. How to Prolong the Happiness of the Marriage Union (1787)

That woman who is unjustly censured by her own sex for a deficiency of good sense, seems to me the best disposed to give comfort in the married state: she is said to want spirit, to be a tame, helpless, dispassionate creature, that she is a sad manager, and would quickly undo her husband. The construction of this is, that she has too much good understanding to thwart and perplex her husband in affairs, which she is sensible he knows much better; that as she has the discernment to discover a much larger capacity in him, she therefore implicitly yields up her own judgment to the stronger mind, and that she has observed, that nothing is gained in the main of life, by saving a little money, through mean and narrow practices. She never rebukes you for want of rectitude, never upbraids you with infidelity; she submits with a becoming easiness to the little turns of your temper, which unlucky accidents in

the world have occasioned; she construes every chagrin in the good na-
tured sense; and while she is fearful of offending, her fondness proceeds
from love and not from duty. Who would not be contented under the
imputation of having married a fool, when blessed with such a woman,
to bring pleasure and comfort to his arms all his vacant hours![12]

Another thing that is very material to promote and prolong the marriage union, is the conduct of the husband to the wife. In the first place,
it is requisite to behave with good manners and decency, with the same
carefulness and regard that a man approaches, his chaste mistress; to let
fall no indelicate expressions, to use no unseemly actions, or to communicate any affairs to her, that may induce her to suspect his honour, or
that shall discover any contempt he has suffered, for women's affections
are generally governed by the opinion of the world. To be a thorough
master of wedlock, it is necessary sometimes to impose upon your wife:
be sure then you make her believe you put a vast confidence in her, that
there is nothing of that great consequence but you would repose in her
bosom; for women will forgive you any thing sooner than your mis-
trusting their fidelity. But, however, you will soon understand, that you
are to entrust them with very few things; for some sudden starts of passion, or weakness, or their love to communicate what they know, will
force a disclosure of the secret. Overlook many trivial errors, regarding
her as a woman, and if she performs any little meritorious action, remember to be thoroughly sensible of it; for women always lay great
stress upon outward, ceremonious behaviour. If you happen, after all, to
love her with passion, your quiet will be very much endangered, and
these rules will be insignificant. You will deviate so far from the prudent
behaviour of a husband to a wife, that she will soon loose her con-
formable disposition, and acquire such fantastic humours and obstinacy
from never being controuled, that eventually all the seeds of affection
will be eradicated, or your total happiness destroyed.

DISCUSSION QUESTIONS

1. How does each author describe marriage? Do both authors believe that
   men should marry? If so, why?
2. Compare and contrast the authors' opinions of women. To what extent
   are the authors' descriptions of the husband's ideal role derived from
   their attitudes toward women?

3. Compare and contrast the style and tone adopted by each of these authors. Why do you think that the author of the second document, "How to Prolong the Happiness of the Marriage Union," is so extravagantly misogynistic?

G. Educating American Youth

Many Americans believed that education was the key to creating the stable and virtuous society they deemed essential to the success of their republican experiment. Educational reformers, such Pennsylvania's Benjamin Rush, author of the Plan for the Establishment of Public Schools, *part of which is reprinted below, believed that popular government required an informed citizenry and envisioned schools as social laboratories that could produce public-spirited citizens. More Americans, however, saw education in a vastly different light, pursuing self-improvement as a means to upward mobility. The second document, which appeared in the* Columbian Magazine, *tells the story of the "Countryman" and illustrates this latter view.*

1. PLAN FOR THE ESTABLISHMENT OF PUBLIC SCHOOLS (1786)

Next to the duty which young men owe to their Creator, I wish to see a SUPREME REGARD TO THEIR COUNTRY inculcated upon them . . . Our

(*Opposite, top*) *The Copley Family*, by John Singleton Copley, 1776–1777. The increasing popularity of family portraits attested to changing attitudes toward domestic life in the eighteenth-century Atlantic world. This painting presents a notably informal and affectionate family circle that includes the artist (gazing outward to engage his audience), his wife and children, and his father. A native of Massachusetts, Copley settled in London in 1774. Andrew W. Mellon Fund. Image © National Gallery of Art, Washington.

(*Opposite, bottom*) *The Washington Family*, by Edward Savage, 1789–1796. This iconic depiction of Washington with his wife, Martha, her grandchildren, and an enslaved African American servant, conveys the importance of domestic relationships while nonetheless depicting a more hierarchical family ideal. Washington is clearly the head of this emotionally reserved household, whose members proffer the sword, maps, and other trappings of the great man's public roles. Andrew W. Mellon Collection. Image © National Gallery of Art, Washington.

country includes family, friends, and property, and should be preferred to them all. Let our pupil be taught that he does not belong to himself, but that he is public property. Let him be taught to love his family, but let him be taught at the same time that he must forsake and even forget them when the welfare of his country requires it.[13]

He must watch for the state as if its liberties depended upon his vigilance alone, but he must do this in such a manner as not to defraud his creditors or neglect his family. He must love private life, but he must decline no station, however public or responsible it may be, when called to it by the suffrages of his fellow citizens. He must love popularity, but he must despise it when set in competition with the dictates of his judgment or the real interest of his country. He must love character and have a due sense of injuries, but he must be taught to appeal only to the laws of the state, to defend the one and punish the other. He must love family honor, but he must be taught that neither the rank nor antiquity of his ancestors can command respect without personal merit. He must avoid neutrality in all questions that divide the state, but he must shun the rage and acrimony of party spirit. He must be taught to love his fellow creatures in every part of the world, but he must cherish with a more intense and peculiar affection the citizens of [his state] and of the United States. . . .

While we inculcate these republican duties upon our pupil, we must not neglect, at the same time, to inspire him with republican principles. He must be taught that there can be no durable liberty but in a republic, and that government, like all other sciences, is of a progressive nature. The chains which have bound this science in Europe are happily unloosed in America. Here it is open to investigation and improvement. While philosophy has protected us by its discoveries from a thousand natural evils, government has unhappily followed with an unequal pace. It would be to dishonour human genius, only to name the many defects which still exist in the best systems of legislation. We daily see matter of a perishable nature rendered durable by certain chemical operations. In like manner, I conceive, that it is possible to combine power in such a way as not only to encrease the happiness, but to promote the duration of republican forms of government far beyond the terms limited for them by history, or the common opinions of mankind. . . .

From the observations that have been made it is plain that I consider it possible to convert men into republican machines. This must be done if we expect them to perform their parts properly in the great machine of the government of the state. That republic is sophisticated with monarchy or aristocracy that does not revolve upon the wills of the people, and these must be fitted to each other by means of education before they can be made to produce regularity and in unison with government.

2. THE PROGRESS OF A COUNTRYMAN (1787)

I was born and educated about eighty miles distance from the city, and, 'till lately, considered myself as a first rate personage. My age is not quite 25. It is true, I have spent the whole of my life, except the last month, in the country—but I was there thought a prodigy . . . My relations kept me at school 'till I was almost twenty-one, and I could then beat my master at figures. It was a lucky thing for me that he died soon after, for I got his place by it, and continued keeping school there 'till a few months ago; when, tired of so insignificant a post, and wishing to signalize myself, I took up the resolution of coming to the city. Preparatory to this, I took every step to qualify myself for acting in the capacity of a clerk in a merchant's counting house; not doubting, but that by my merits, I should at least rise to be cashier of the bank . . . I shall not trouble you with the particulars of my journey—all went on very well 'till I arrived in the city. My treatment there was rather mortifying. My horse was none of the best, it is true, for he was about twelve hands high, and had lost one of his ears, which neighbour Spriggins cut off, because he had trespassed on his ground. As I proceeded slowly through the street, viewing the various objects that presented, I was frequently put out of countenance by the remarks I heard made. . . .[14]

The next day, after a vast deal of trouble, I found out a cousin of mine, who had been in town a year or two, and was apprentice to a hatter: he being a great beau, and a lad of spirit, agreed to show me the city, and initiate me into its mysteries. We patrolled all the streets, and saw every thing worth seeing. The recapitulation would, to you, be tedious and dull, but I was pleased and delighted. The language that I heard uttered from different parts, during our walks, was many times unintelligible; and, indeed, such as my conductor could not always explain. . . .

We next went to the court-house, for I had heard a great deal about lawyers, and wished to hear them speak: upon going up the steps, I observed a number of young gentlemen, with their hair as white as new cheese, spread out like a half bushel, with a sort of spy-glasses in their hands, which they looked through every minute; (this I suppose was to sharpen their wit, for it made them look very fierce). I staid at the court-house almost two hours, and the chief part of what I heard, was "may it please your honour"; and then they would read passages as long as my arm out of their big books; and which I was told had nothing to do with the subject. They strutted so often by me, and pulled out their spy-glasses so frequently, that I was glad when my cousin agreed to leave the place.

We next passed by the coffee-house, for I expected the merchants would be talking on the good of the nation; but I could hear little but discourses about roast beef, oysters, and bills of exchange. However, as my business was to be with this class of men, I pleased myself with the prospect of good living.

I have not yet been able to get a place, but have employed myself in improving my dress and person; and by the assistance of my cousin make now a pretty genteel appearance. I wear three glass seals, of different colours, that cost me two shillings and six pence a piece, to my old watch, and have my head dressed by a barber. Moreover, I intend to learn to dance, and talk of going to the next concert.

DISCUSSION QUESTIONS

1. What did Rush mean when he characterized the citizen as "public property"? What did he mean when he said that he hoped to "convert men into republican machines" by virtue of education? Would any of Royall Tyler's characters in *The Contrast* have accepted Rush's views?

2. Do you think that the author of "The Progress of a Countryman" would have agreed with Rush's views on education and its uses?

3. "The Progress of a Countryman" was published about a month before Tyler wrote *The Contrast*. What common themes do these two pieces share? Which piece presents the more optimistic outlook for the future of America?

H. The Meaning of Equality

Enshrined in the Declaration of Independence, the idea of equality was much debated among post-revolutionary Americans. While contemporaries typically confined their discussions of political equality to white men alone, even then they disagreed on the extent to which the common man should wield political power. The first selection, below, is an excerpt from Modern Chivalry, *a novel by Hugh Henry Brackenridge in which characters disagree about what sorts of men are fit to hold political office. The second document, written in 1813, is a famous letter in which an aging Thomas Jefferson expounded to his friend and fellow revolutionary John Adams on what he considered the uniquely American ideal of a "natural aristocracy."*

1. THE WILL OF THE PEOPLE (1792)

The Captain rising early next morning, and setting out on his way, had now arrived at a place where a number of people were convened, for the purpose of electing persons to represent them in the legislature of the state. There was a weaver who was a candidate for this appointment, and seemed to have a good deal of interest among the people. But another, who was a man of education was his competitor. Relying on some talent of speaking which he thought he possessed, he addressed the multitude.[15]

Fellow citizens, said he, I pretend not to any great abilities; but am conscious to myself that I have the best good will to serve you. But it is very astonishing to me, that this weaver should conceive himself qualified for the trust. For though my acquirements are not great, yet his are still less. The mechanical business which he pursues, must necessarily take up so much of his time, that he cannot apply himself to political studies. I should therefore think it would be more answerable to your dignity, and conducive to your interest, to be represented by a man at least of some letters, than by an illiterate handicraftsman like this. It will be more honourable for himself, to remain at his loom and knot threads, than to come forward in a legislative capacity; because in the one case, he is in the sphere suited to his education; in the other, he is like a fish out of water, and must struggle for breath in a new element.

Is it possible he can understand the affairs of government, whose mind has been concentered to the small object of weaving webs, to the price by the yard, the grist of the thread, and such like matters as concern the manufacturer of cloths? The feet of him who weaves, are more occupied than the head, or at least as much; and therefore he must be, at least, but in half, accustomed to exercise his mental powers. For these reasons, all other things set aside, the chance is in my favour, with respect to information. However, you will decide, and give your suffrages to him or to me, as you shall judge expedient.

The Captain hearing these observations, and looking at the weaver, could not help advancing, and undertaking to subjoin something in support of what had been just said. Said he, I have no prejudice against a weaver more than another man . . . But to rise from the cellar to the senate house, would be an unnatural hoist. To come from counting threads, and adjusting them to the splits of a reed, to regulate the finances of a government, would be preposterous; there being no congruity in the case. There is no analogy between knotting threads and framing laws. It would be a reversion of the order of things. Not that a manufacturer of linen or woolen, or other stuff, is an inferior character, but a different one, from that which ought to be employed in affairs of state. It is unnecessary to enlarge on this subject; for you must all be convinced of the truth and propriety of what I say. But if you will give me leave to take the manufacturer aside a little, I think I can explain to him my ideas on the subject; and very probably prevail with him to withdraw his pretensions. The people seeming to acquiesce, and beckoning to the weaver, they withdrew aside, and the Captain addressed him in the following words:

Mr. Traddle, said he, for that was the name of the manufacturer, I have not the smallest idea of wounding your sensibility; but it would seem to me, it would be more your interest to pursue your occupation, than to launch out into that of which you have no knowledge. When you go to the senate house, the application to you will not be to warp a web; but to make laws for the commonwealth. Now, suppose that the making these laws, requires a knowledge of commerce, or of the interests of agriculture, or those principles upon which the different manufactures depend, what service could you render? It is possible you might think justly enough; but could you speak? You are not in the habit of public speaking. You are not furnished with those common place ideas with which even very ignorant men can pass for knowing something. There is nothing makes a man so ridiculous as to attempt what is above his sphere. You are no tumbler for instance; yet should you give out that you could vault upon a man's back; or turn heels over head, like the wheels of a cart; the stiffness of your joints would encumber you; and you would fall upon your posteriors to the ground. Such a squash as that, would do you damage. The getting up to ride on the state is an unsafe thing to those who are not accustomed to such horsemanship. It is a disagreeable thing for a man to be laughed at, and there is no way of keeping one's self from it but by avoiding all affectation.

While they were thus discoursing, a bustle had taken place among the crowd. Teague [the Captain's Irish servant] hearing so much about elections, and serving the government, took it into his head, that he could be a legislator himself. The thing was not displeasing to the people, who seemed to favour his pretensions; owing, in some degree, to there being several of his countrymen among the crowd; but more especially to the fluctuation of the popular mind, and a disposition to what is new and ignoble. For though the weaver was not the most elevated object of choice, yet he was still preferable to this tatter-demalion, who was but a menial servant, and had so much of what is called the brogue on his tongue, as to fall far short of an elegant speaker.

The Captain coming up, and finding what was on the carpet, was greatly chagrined at not having been able to give the multitude a better idea of the importance of a legislative trust; alarmed also, from an apprehension of the loss of his servant. Under these impressions he resumed his address to the multitude. Said he, this is making the matter still worse, gentlemen: this servant of mine is but a bog-trotter, who can scarcely speak the dialect in which your laws ought to be written; but certainly has never read a single treatise on any political subject; for the truth is, he cannot read at all . . . A free government is a noble acquisition to a people: and this freedom consists in an equal right to make laws, and to have the benefit of the laws when made. Though doubtless, in such a government, the lowest citizen may become chief magistrate; yet it is sufficient to possess the right, not absolutely necessary to exercise it. Or even if you should think proper, now and then, to show your privilege, and exert, in a signal manner, the democratic prerogative, yet is it not descending too low to filch away from me a hireling, which I cannot well spare? You are surely carrying the matter too far, in thinking to make a senator of this ostler; to take him away from an employment to which he has been bred, and put him to another, to which he has served no apprenticeship: to set those hands which have been lately employed in currying my horse, to the draughting-bills, and preparing business for the house.

The people were tenacious of their choice, and insisted on giving Teague their suffrages; and by the frown upon their brows, seemed to indicate resentment at what had been said; as indirectly charging them with want of judgment; or calling in question their privilege to do what they thought proper. It is a very strange thing, said one of them, who was a speaker for the rest, that after having conquered Burgoyne and Cornwallis, and got a government of our own, we cannot put in it whom we please. This young man may be your servant, or another man's servant: but if we chuse to make him a delegate, what is that to you? He may not be yet skilled in the matter, but there is a good day coming. We will empower him; and it is better to trust a plain man like him, than one of your high flyers, that will make laws to suit their own purposes.

I had much rather, said the Captain, you would send the weaver, though I thought that improper, than to invade my household, and thus detract from me the very person that I have about me to brush my boots, and clean my spurs. The prolocutor of the people gave him to understand that his objections were useless, for the people had determined on the choice, and Teague they would have, for a representative.

Finding it answered no end to expostulate with the multitude, he requested to speak a word with Teague by himself. Stepping aside, he said to him, composing his voice, and addressing him in a soft manner: Teague you are quite wrong in this matter they have put into your head. Do you know what it is to be a member of a deliberative body? What qualifications are necessary? Do you understand any thing of geography? If a question should be put to make a law to dig a canal in some part of the state, can you describe the bearing of the mountains, and the course of the rivers? Or if commerce is to be pushed to some new quarter, by the force of regulations, are you competent to decide in such a case? There will be questions of law, and astronomy on the carpet. How you must gape and stare like a fool, when you come to be asked your opinion on these subjects! Are you acquainted with the abstract principles of finance; with the funding public securities; the ways and means of raising the revenue; providing for the discharge of the public debts, and all other things which respect the economy of the government? Even if you had knowledge, have you a facility of speaking? I would suppose you would have too much pride to go to the house just to say, ay, or no. This is not the fault of your nature, but of your education; having been accustomed to dig turf in your early years, rather than instructing yourself in the classics, or common school books.

When a man becomes a member of a public body, he is like a racoon, or other beast that climbs up the fork of a tree; the boys pushing at him with pitchforks, or throwing stones or shooting at him with an arrow, the dogs barking in the mean time. One will find fault with your not speaking; another with your speaking, if you speak at all. They will put you in the newspapers, and ridicule you as a perfect beast. There is what they call the caricatura; that is, representing you with a dog's head, or a cat's claw. As you have a red head, they will very probably make a fox of you, or a sorrel horse, or a brindled cow. It is the devil in hell to be exposed to the squibs and crackers of the gazette wits and publications. You know no more about these matters than a goose; and yet you would undertake rashly, without advice, to enter on the office; nay, contrary to advice . . . You have nothing but your character, Teague, in a new country to depend upon. Let it never be said, that you quitted an honest livelihood, the taking care of my horse, to follow the new fangled whims of the times, and be a statesman.

Teague was moved chiefly with the last part of the address, and consented to relinquish his pretensions.

The Captain, glad of this, took him back to the people, and announced his disposition to decline the honour which they had intended him.

Teague acknowledged that he had changed his mind, and was willing to remain in a private station.

The people did not seem well pleased with the Captain; but as nothing more could be said about the matter, they turned their attention to the weaver, and gave him their suffrages.

2. The Natural Aristocracy (1813)

I agree with you that there is a natural aristocracy among men. The grounds of this are virtue and talents. Formerly, bodily powers gave place among the *aristoi*. But since the invention of gunpowder has armed the weak as well as the strong with missile death, bodily strength, like beauty, good humor, politeness and other accomplishments, has become but an auxiliary ground for distinction. There is also an artificial aristocracy, founded on wealth and birth, without either virtue or talents; for with these it would belong to the first class. The natural aristocracy I consider as the most precious gift of nature, for the instruction, the trusts, and government of society. And indeed, it would have been inconsistent in creation to have formed man for the social state, and not to have provided virtue and wisdom enough to manage the concerns of the society. May we not even say, that that form of government is the best, which provides the most effectually for a pure selection of these natural *aristoi* into the offices of government? The artificial aristocracy is a mischievous ingredient in government, and provision should be made to prevent its ascendency. . . .[16]

At the first session of our [Virginia] legislature after the Declaration of Independence, we passed a law abolishing entails. And this was followed by one abolishing the privilege of primogeniture, and dividing the lands of intestates equally among all their children, or other representatives. These [inheritance reform] laws, drawn by myself, laid the ax to the foot of pseudoaristocracy. And had another which I prepared been adopted by the legislature, our work would have been complete. It was a bill for the more general diffusion of learning. This proposed to divide every county into wards of five or six miles square, like your townships; to establish in each ward a free school for reading, writing and common arithmetic; to provide for the annual selection of the best subjects from these schools, who might receive, at the public expense, a higher degree of education at a district school; and from these district schools to select a certain number of the most promising subjects, to be completed at an University, where all the useful sciences should be taught. Worth and genius would thus have been sought out from every condition of life, and completely prepared by education for defeating the competition of wealth and birth for public trusts . . . The law for religious freedom, which made a part of this system, having put down the aristocracy of the clergy, and restored to the citizen the freedom of the mind, and those of entails and descents nurturing an equality of condition among them, this on education would have raised the mass of the people to the high ground of moral respectability necessary to their own safety, and to orderly government; and would have completed the great object of qualifying them to select the veritable *aristoi*, for the trusts of government, to the exclusion of the pseudalists . . . Although this law has not yet been acted on but in a small and inefficient degree, it is still considered as before the legislature, with other bills of the revised code, not yet taken up, and I have great hope that some patriotic spirit will, at a favorable moment, call it up, and make it the key-stone of the arch of our government.

DISCUSSION QUESTIONS

1. In the election scene from *Modern Chivalry,* Brackenridge's characters differ in their understanding of the meaning of equality in post-revolutionary America. What conflicting opinions do the Captain, the weaver, the crowd, and Teague express? With whom do you think the author's sympathies lie—and why?

2. What do we know about the political ideals of the characters in *The Contrast?* With which of Brackenridge's characters might Colonel Manly or Billy Dimple agree? Which of Brackenridge's characters expressed opinions that might have found favor with Maria, Jonathan, or Jessamy?

3. What is a "natural aristocracy" and how, according to Jefferson, might Americans promote it? Since "aristocracy" means the rule of few, did support for a natural aristocracy necessarily presuppose rejecting the ideal of equality?

NOTES

1. "The Former, Present, and Future Prospects of America," *Columbian Magazine,* 1 (Oct. 1786): 84–85.

2. Augustus Dabbler, "Proposals for Taking a Literary Associate," *Columbian Magazine,* 2 (Apr. 1788): 206–8.

3. [William Haliburton], *Effects of the Stage on the Manners of a People: and the Propriety of Encouraging and Establishing a Virtuous Theatre* (Boston: Young and Etheridge, 1792), 9–11, 14–15, 17–18, 25.

4. *Copy of a Petition now circulating for Subscription, humbly offered for the Perusal of the Members of the Honourable House of Assembly* (Philadelphia, 1793), at http://memory.loc.gov/cgi-bin/query/r?ammem/rbpe:@field(DOCID+@lit(rbpe16301100)), [accessed 3 Mar. 2006].

5. Chesterfield to his son, 16 Oct. 1747, in Bonamy Dobrée, ed., *The Letters of Philip Dormer Stanhope, 4th Earl of Chesterfield,* 6 vols. (London: Eyre and Spottiswoode, 1932), 3:1035–38.

6. M[ercy] W[arren], "Criticism on Chesterfield's Letters," *Massachusetts Magazine,* 2 (Jan. 1790): 36–38. See also Edmund M. Hayes, "Mercy Otis War-

ren versus Lord Chesterfield, 1779," *William and Mary Quarterly,* 3rd ser. 40 (1983): 616–21.

7. Republican, "For the Females," [New York] *Daily Advertiser,* 17 Apr. 1787.

8. A Republican, "For the *Daily Advertiser,*" [New York] *Daily Advertiser,* 18 Apr. 1787.

9. A Matrimonial Republican, "On Matrimonial Obedience," *Lady's Magazine, and Repository of Entertaining Knowledge,* 1 (July 1792): 64–66.

10. Samuel K. Jennings, *The Married Lady's Companion,* 2nd ed. (1804; New York: Lorenzo Dow, 1808), 61–66.

11. "Panegyric on the Marriage State," *Columbian Magazine,* 1 (Oct. 1786): 71–74.

12. Benedict, "How to Prolong the Happiness of the Marriage Union" *Columbian Magazine,* 1 (June 1787): 474–75.

13. Benjamin Rush, *Plan for the Establishment of Public Schools and the Diffusion of Knowledge in Pennsylvania* (Philadelphia: Thomas Dobson, 1786), 20–23, 27.

14. John Clodman, "The Progress of a Countryman," *Columbian Magazine,* 1 (Mar. 1787): 314–16.

15. Hugh Henry Brackenridge, *Modern Chivalry: Containing the Adventures of Captain John Ferrago and Teague O'Regan, his servant,* 4 vols. (Philadelphia: John M'Culloch, 1792–97), 1:25–36.

16. Thomas Jefferson to John Adams, 28 Oct. 1813, in Paul Leicester Ford, ed., *The Works of Thomas Jefferson,* 12 vols. (New York: G. P. Putnam's Sons, 1904–5), 11:343–48.

Suggested Reading

This bibliography includes a selection of useful readings on overlapping themes and topics pertaining to Royall's Tyler's *The Contrast* and the political and cultural history of revolutionary America.

ARTS AND LITERATURE

Agnew, Jean-Christophe. *Worlds Apart: The Market and the Theater in Anglo-American Thought, 1550–1750*. Cambridge, Eng.: Cambridge University Press, 1986.

Davidson, Cathy N. *Revolution and the Word: The Rise of the Novel in America*. New York: Oxford University Press, 1986.

Dunlap, William. *A History of the American Theatre from Its Origins to 1832*, ed. Tice L. Miller. 1832; Urbana: University of Illinois Press, 2005.

Elliott, Emory. *Revolutionary Writers: Literature and Authority in the New Republic, 1725–1810*. New York: Oxford University Press, 1982.

Ellis, Joseph J. *After the Revolution: Profiles of Early American Culture*. New York: W. W. Norton, 1979.

Kornfeld, Eve. *Creating an American Culture: A Brief History with Documents*. New York: Bedford/St. Martin's, 2001.

Lovell, Margaretta M. *Art In a Season of Revolution: Painters, Artisans, and Patrons in Early America*. Philadelphia: University of Pennsylvania Press, 2005.

Meserve, Walter J. *An Emerging Entertainment: The Drama of the American People to 1828*. Bloomington: Indiana University Press, 1977.

Newton, Sarah Emily. "Wise and Foolish Virgins: 'Usable Fiction' and the Early American Conduct Tradition." *Early American Literature,* 25 (1990): 139–67.

Richards, Jeffrey H. *Drama, Theater, and Identity in the American New Republic*. Cambridge, Eng.: Cambridge University Press, 2005.

Schwartz, Barry. *George Washington: The Making of an American Symbol*. Ithaca, N.Y.: Cornell University Press, 1987.

Silverman, Kenneth. *A Cultural History of the American Revolution*. New York: Crowell, 1976.

Tompkins, Jane. *Sensational Designs: The Cultural Work of American Fiction, 1790–1860*. New York: Oxford University Press, 1986.

Wood, Gordon S. *The Rising Glory of America, 1760–1820*. 1971; Boston: Northeastern University Press, 1990.

GENDER AND FAMILY

Barker-Benfield, G. J. *The Culture of Sensibility: Sex and Society in Eighteenth-Century Britain*. Chicago: University of Chicago Press, 1992.

Bloch, Ruth H. "American Feminine Ideals in Transition: The Rise of the Moral Mother." *Feminist Studies*, 4 (1978): 101–26.

———. "The Gendered Meanings of Virtue in Revolutionary America." *Signs*, 13 (1987):37–58.

Chrisman, Kimberly. "Unhoop the Fair Sex: The Campaign Against the Hoop Petticoat in Eighteenth-Century England." *Eighteenth-Century Studies*, 30 (1996): 5–23.

Greven, Philip J. *The Protestant Temperament: Patterns of Child-Rearing, Religious Experience, and the Self in Early America*. New York: Alfred A. Knopf, 1977.

Jabour, Anya. *Marriage in the Early Republic: Elizabeth and William Wirt and the Companionate Ideal*. Baltimore: Johns Hopkins University Press, 1998.

Kann, Mark E. *A Republic of Men: The American Founders, Gendered Language, and Patriarchal Politics*. New York: New York University Press, 1998.

Kerber, Linda K. *Women of the Republic: Intellect and Ideology in Early America*. Chapel Hill: University of North Carolina Press, 1980.

Kerrison, Catherine. "By the Book: Eliza Ambler Brent Carrington and Conduct Literature in Late Eighteenth-Century Virginia." *Virginia Magazine of History and Biography*, 105 (1997): 27–52.

———. "The Novel as Teacher: Learning to be Female in the Early American South." *Journal of Southern History*, 69 (2003): 513–48.

Knott, Sarah. "Sensibility and the American War of Independence." *American Historical Review*, 109 (2004): 19–40.

Lewis, Jan. *The Pursuit of Happiness: Family and Values in Jefferson's Virginia*. Cambridge, Eng.: Cambridge University Press, 1983.

———. "The Republican Wife: Virtue and Seduction in the Early Republic." *William and Mary Quarterly*, 3rd ser., 44 (1987): 689–712.

Stansell, Christine. *City of Women: Sex and Class in New York, 1789–1860*. Urbana: University of Illinois Press, 1987.

Wahrman, Dror. *The Making of the Modern Self: Identity and Culture in Eighteenth-Century England*. New Haven, Conn.: Yale University Press, 2004.

Zagarri, Rosemarie. "Morals, Manners, and the Republican Mother." *American Quarterly*, 44 (1992): 192–215.

POLITICS AND SOCIETY

Allgor, Catherine. *Parlor Politics: In Which the Ladies of Washington Help Build a City and a Government.* Charlottesville: University Press of Virginia, 2000.

Appleby, Joyce. *Capitalism and a New Social Order: The Republican Vision of the 1790s.* New York: New York University Press, 1984.

Bushman, Richard L. *The Refinement of America: Persons, Houses, Cities.* New York: Alfred A. Knopf, 1992.

Fliegelman, Jay. *Prodigals and Pilgrims: The American Revolution against Patriarchal Authority.* Cambridge, Eng.: Cambridge University Press, 1982.

Gross, Robert A., ed. *In Debt to Shays: The Bicentennial of an Agrarian Rebellion.* Charlottesville: University Press of Virginia, 1993.

Hemphill, C. Dallett. *Bowing to Necessities: A History of Manners in America, 1620–1860.* New York: Oxford University Press, 1999.

Hodges, Graham Russell. *Root and Branch: African Americans in New York and New Jersey, 1613–1863.* Chapel Hill: University of North Carolina Press, 1999.

Kloppenberg, James. "The Virtues of Liberalism: Christianity, Republicanism, and Ethics in Early American Political Discourse." *Journal of American History,* 74 (1987): 9–33.

McCoy, Drew. *The Elusive Republic: Political Economy in Jeffersonian America.* Chapel Hill: University of North Carolina Press, 1980.

Richards, Leonard L. *Shays's Rebellion: The American Revolution's Final Battle.* Philadelphia: University of Pennsylvania Press, 2002.

Szatmary, David P. *Shay's Rebellion: The Making of an Agrarian Insurrection.* Amherst: University of Massachusetts Press, 1980.

Withington, Ann Fairfax. *Toward a More Perfect Union: Virtue and the Formation of American Republics.* New York: Oxford University Press, 1991.

Wood, Gordon S. *The Radicalism of the American Revolution.* New York: Alfred A. Knopf, 1991.

ROYALL TYLER

Carson, Ada Lou and Herbert L. Carson. *Royall Tyler.* Boston: Twayne, 1979.

Evelev, John. "*The Contrast:* The Problem of Theatricality and Political and Social Crisis in Postrevolutionary America." *Early American Literature,* 31 (1996): 74–97.

Pressman, Richard S. "Class Positioning and Shays' Rebellion: Resolving the Contradictions of *The Contrast.*" *Early American Literature,* 21 (1986): 87–102.

Siebert, Donald T. "Royall Tyler's 'Bold Example': *The Contrast* and the English Comedy of Manners." *Early American Literature,* 13 (1978): 3–11.

Tanselle, G. Thomas. *Royall Tyler*. Cambridge, Mass.: Harvard University Press, 1967.

Tyler, Mary Palmer. *Grandmother Tyler's Book: The Recollections of Mary Palmer Tyler,* ed. Helen Tyler Brown and Frederick Tupper. New York: Putnam, 1925.

Index